1999

IN HONORED GLORY

ARLINGTON NATIONAL CEMETERY
THE FINAL POST

THIRD EDITION

Philip Bigler

VANDAMERE
PRESS

Published by
Vandamere Press
P.O. Box 17446
Clearwater, FL 33762
USA

Third Edition
Copyright 1999 by Vandamere Press

First Edition Printing History

First Printing December, 1986
Second Printing August, 1987
Third Printing April, 1990
Fourth Printing April, 1992

Second Edition Printing History

First Printing May, 1994
Second Printing May, 1996
Third Printing July, 1997
Fourth Printing September, 1998

Third Edition Printing History

First Printing May, 1999
Second Printing June, 2000
Third Printing January, 2001
Fourth Printing September, 2001

ISBN 0-918339-47-2, hardcover
ISBN 0-918339-48-0, paper

Manufactured in the United States of America.

ACKNOWLEDGMENTS

I would like to take this opportunity to express my thanks to the many individuals who provided assistance during the preparation of this book. First, I am indebted to Raymond J. Costanzo, the former Superintendent of Arlington National Cemetery, who graciously gave his time and support to this project. I am especially grateful for the assistance of the Historian's Office at Arlington. Tom Sherlock, my co-worker for two years and my good friend, provided much of the inspiration for this book and he selflessly offered both his personal time and advice during these past months. Tom remains probably the greatest single source on the history of Arlington Cemetery. Historian Kerri Childress has similarly been exceedingly helpful and patient in assisting with the research for *In Honored Glory* as has Kathryn Shenkle who checked this work for accuracy and who made suggestions for improvements for the second edition. I would like to acknowledge both Thurmon Higginbotham and Gene Wilson who freely reminisced about their rich careers at Arlington.

LTC John Myers and Ms. Shari Lawrence at the Army Public Affairs Office at Fort McNair have been of invaluable assistance and this work could not have been finished without their generous contributions. Patty Heard and SGT Jay Larson likewise were kind to assist me with arranging interviews with the caisson platoon at Fort Myer. I would also like to thank the other branches of the armed services who have provide material for this book and, in particular, LTC Joseph Wagovich, USAF, for his assistance.

The sentinels at the Tomb of the Unknown Soldier deserve special recognition and acknowledgment. My thanks go to S/SGT Ken Gordon and SP4 Brett Gookin. At the caisson platoon, 1SGT Michael Wilson was an outstanding resource in relating the history and duties of the regiment.

At the John F. Kennedy Library, I am similarly indebted to Mr. Dave Powers who shared with me some of his memories of the President. Also, thanks to Jim Cedrone and James Hill for their help in conducting photographic research at the Library. At the National Geographic Society, Caroline Sakel and Leah Roberts provided many excellent resources on Peary's Arctic expeditions and on Matthew Henson's crucial role in the discovery of the North Pole.

My editor, Pat Berger, and my publisher, Art Brown, have worked diligently with me. Their suggestions and comments have been greatly welcomed and appreciated. Special thanks also to Jerry Dreo for his work on the cover photo and to Dick Cramer for his timely photographic assistance.

Phil Walsh with the National Park Service has helped me locate key government records and Wende Walsh has graciously provided grammatical advice.

I would like to thank those people who worked on the much-needed index for this new edition: Karen Bierman, Cathy Colglazier, Janna Fox, Karen Lockard, Tom Mulhearn, and Carole Mulhearn.

Finally, I would be remiss if I did not acknowledge several special people who have provided much needed encouragement during these past months. My wife, Linda, has been an exceptional proofreader, a loving friend, and an understanding spouse. My father, Charles Bigler, has been lovingly supportive and a constant inspiration.

Since the first writing of this book, my mother, Bernice Bigler, has passed away and is now buried at Arlington just below the Tomb of the Unknown Soldier. Her death continues to serves as a daily reminder to me of the importance of Arlington National Cemetery and of its special place in our nation's heritage. It is my hope that this book will serve to honor her and all of our military families while providing some solace to those who continue to mourn our nation's sons and daughters.

TABLE OF CONTENTS

Chapter 1 7
The Nation's Burial Ground

Chapter 2 11
[A] Most Pleasant and Healthful Place

Chapter 3 23
Your Old Home Has . . . Been Desecrated

Chapter 4 41
Where Valor Proudly Sleeps

Chapter 5 61
Under My Eternal Vigilance

Chapter 6 79
Your Sons and Daughters Have Served You Well

Chapter 7 89
The Torch Has Been Passed

Chapter 8 105
May God Cradle You in His Loving Arms

Chapter 9 121
Beyond the Stars

Appendix A 131
Notable Names and Burial Locations

Appendix B 136
Arlington Chronology

Appendix C 141
Inscriptions at the Kennedy Gravesite

Appendix D 144
Eligibility Requirements and Stone Markings

Appendix E 148
Twenty-one Facts About Arlington Cemetery

Appendix F 151
The Caisson Platoon

Bibliography 155

Index 157

Dedicated to the memory
of
BERNICE R. BIGLER

Whose life daily reflected the
dedication, sacrifice, and patriotism
of our nation's military families.

October 27, 1920–February 28, 1989   Section 7A, 113

In Memoriam

Major Otho Leroy Mimms
United States Air Force
Section 7, 9198-A

Col. Paul J. Walsh
United States Army
Section 60, 1435

MSgt. Fred Fisher
United States Marine Corps
Section 13, 14456

Evelyn Inez Dunson
Section 7, 10185-B

CHAPTER ONE

The Nation's Burial Ground

Each morning, the serenity of Arlington National Cemetery is temporarily interrupted by the sharp report of rifle volleys followed by the haunting notes of "Taps." An Armed Forces casket team quickly folds an outstretched American flag into a triangle which is solemnly presented to a next of kin. The identical ceremony is repeated throughout the day, the nation's final tribute to its deceased veterans.

Arlington National Cemetery was carved out of the 1,100-acre plantation originally owned by George Washington Parke Custis and is now the most widely known of the 109 operating national cemeteries. Over 260,000 Americans are buried within the grounds—the famous and the anonymous, generals and privates, presidents and politicians.

Overlooking the cemetery's 612 acres is the majestic, classical-revival Arlington House mansion, the antebellum home of the Confederate general, Robert E. Lee. Built in the early 19th century, the manor house was seized at the outset of the American Civil War. It was initially converted into a military headquarters for the Union Army but in 1864, in an act of vengeance, burials were begun around the mansion to prevent Lee from ever returning to his beloved home.

Nearby are endless rows of identical white headstones, marking the graves of over 16,000 federal soldiers who lost their lives during the Civil War. Appropriately known as the "Field of the Dead", the section bears a silent testimony to the incredible human toll of the nation's most divisive war. A short distance away, a stark, granite memorial erected over the commingled remains of 2,111 unknowns is further witness to that horrible loss.

U.S. Air Force Photo by O.L. Carlisle

Directly below the Arlington House mansion is the grave of President John F. Kennedy, one of the two American chief executives buried at the cemetery. The focal point of the memorial gravesite is the eternal flame which provides a powerful reminder of the continued legacy of the young President's ideals. Inscribed around the grave's ellipse are inspiring quotations from President Kennedy's 1961 inaugural address. His brother, Robert F. Kennedy, is buried in an adjacent site.

In the distance is the Memorial Amphitheater, once called "America's Temple of Patriotism." The structure was originally built to accommodate the large Memorial Day crowds that annually gathered at the cemetery. Today, the Amphitheater is now intimately associated with the Tomb of the Unknown Soldier, undoubtedly the nation's most sacred shrine to American servicemen. In 1921, the World War I Unknown was buried on the plaza of the Amphitheater and subsequently anonymous soldiers from World War II, the Korean Conflict, and the Vietnam Conflict have similarly been interred, all perpetually guarded by a stoic sentinel from the 3d United States Infantry, "the Old Guard." Some 1,600

U.S. Army Photo

An American serviceman is escorted to his final rest at Arlington National Cemetery.

ceremonies are conducted at the Tomb each year in honor of American soldiers.

Numerous monuments to American servicemen are located throughout Arlington Cemetery. The Mast of the *U.S.S. Maine* was erected near the graves of the sailors who were killed in the catastrophic explosion of the vessel in 1898; the Spanish-American Memorial pays tribute to those who lost their lives in the ensuing war with Spain. The Confederate Memorial commemorates the valor of Southern soldiers during the Civil War while the Argonne Cross represents members of the American Expeditionary Forces which liberated Europe during World War I.

Arlington has become the final resting place for many notables from American history. Among these are General Philip Sheridan, the Union cavalry commander; General of the Armies John J. "Black Jack" Pershing, the highest ranking American military officer; Joe Louis, the famed heavyweight champion; Earl Warren, the Chief Justice of the Supreme Court; and William Howard Taft, President of the United States. Dead from all of the nation's wars from the Revolution through Vietnam have also been buried at Arlington; soldiers who saw action during the climactic battle of Gettysburg or who landed on the beaches of Normandy or who withstood the brutal siege at Khe Sanh. Others died exploring new realms, including Gus Grissom and Roger Chaffee aboard *Apollo I* and Francis Scobee and Michael Smith on the Space Shuttle *Challenger* . Tragic accidents and catastrophic disasters have similarly conspired to take the lives of other American servicemen—21 Marines in a terrorist bombing in Lebanon; 18 sailors in a fire on the *U.S.S. Forrestal* ; three crewmen in a crash during an aborted rescue effort of American hostages in Iran.

Each year, three and a half million visitors make the pilgrimage to Arlington Cemetery, the nation's most hallowed burial ground. The thousands of Americans who are interred at the cemetery have their names inscribed in stone but their deeds are recorded in the nation's history. Each headstone represents a story waiting to be told, a past to be remembered.

CHAPTER TWO

[A] Most Pleasant and Healthful Place

—Henry Fleete

The American Indians in the Arlington area were known as the Necostins. Their tribal organization was part of the Indian confederation led by Chief Powhatan, whose dominion extended over 30 Algonquin tribes. The Indians had successfully lived in relative prosperity in the region for at least 10,000 years deriving a bountiful existence from the fertile land by cultivating ample amounts of maize [corn], beans, and squash. They also supplemented their food stores through hunting, gathering, and fishing. In addition to their agricultural activity, the Algonquin tribes of Virginia routinely conducted an extensive trade throughout Virginia and much of the East Coast via the inland waterways and through a series of elaborate paths and trails.

In 1608, a year after the tenuous establishment of the Jamestown colony, Captain John Smith led a small band of adventurers up the Chesapeake Bay in search of the mythical passage through the North American continent to the coveted Far Eastern markets of Cipangu [Japan] and Cathay [China]. Instead, the explorers discovered the teeming waters of the Potomac River and continued to sail up to the fall line. Near the present site of Arlington National Cemetery, Captain Smith encountered a series of small Algonquin Indian settlements which he described in his *General History*:

> Their houses are in the midst of their fields or gardens; which are small plots of ground some 20 [acres], some 40, some 100, some 200, some more, some less. Sometimes from 2 to 100 of these houses are together, or but a little separated

by groves of trees. Near their habitations is little small wood,
or old trees on the ground, by reason of their burning them
for fire.

The journey of Captain Smith's party of explorers to the fall line of the
Potomac portended disaster for the Indians of Arlington and, indeed, for
all the tribes of Virginia. The English settlers unknowingly brought to
America new and potent diseases to which the American Indian populations had no natural immunity. Within 50 years, over two-thirds of the
native American population of the colony perished from European epidemics of smallpox, tuberculosis, and pneumonia. The remaining survivors were left weak and ill-equipped to resist the onslaught of English
settlers who were continuing to migrate to America. Ironically, the continued growth of the Virginia Colony was ensured by the Indians who
introduced the English to tobacco. Europeans quickly developed a taste
for the cured leaf, guaranteeing the economic prosperity of the colony.

The early white settlers of Virginia initially hoped to convert the "hea-
then" Indian populations to Christianity, a desire tempered by the crav-
ing for prime land and the colonists' misconception that the Indians were
savage and primitive. These impressions were furthered by the fact that
the Indians of the Chesapeake had yet to domesticate animals and lacked
a knowledge of metallurgy and the wheel. Also they had failed to codify
a written language.

In 1622 and again in 1644, the Powhatan Confederacy attacked the city
of Jamestown and the neighboring English settlements in a desperate
effort to stop the white man's intrusion. Superior English armaments
and technology were sufficient to subdue the hostile tribes. The warfare
led the Virginia settlers increasingly to perceive the natives as an obstacle
to civilization that had to be removed or eradicated. By 1679, the remnant
tribes, including the Necostins of Arlington, had been dislodged from
the lands along the tidal waters of the Potomac and James Rivers and the
Chesapeake Bay. The northern regions of Virginia were finally opened
for settlement.

The majority of English colonists preferred to establish tobacco plantations along the fertile banks of the James River which provided the quick-
est access to the world tobacco markets. Subsequent generations of settlers who migrated to Virginia to seek their fortunes, however, found
that the prime tobacco lands had already been claimed by previous inhabitants and were forced to seek unsettled lands to the north. Henry
Fleete, a fur trapper who had been captured by the Indians of northern
Virginia and who lived in the region for decades, encouraged the colonists to migrate to the Potomac River basin. He noted that, "This place
without all question is the most pleasant and healthful place in all this
country and most convenient for habitation, the air temperate in summer

and not violent in winter . . . as for deer, buffaloes, bears, turkeys, the woods do swarm with them and the soil is exceedingly fertile."

In 1669, William Berkeley, the royal governor of Virginia, bestowed a substantial northern land grant of 6,000 acres to Captain Robert Howsing in compensation for the large number of settlers he had transported to the labor-starved colony. The land, located along the Potomac River, included the current site of Arlington National Cemetery. Howsing had no intention of leaving the sea to become a Virginia planter; instead, he immediately sold the property to John Alexander for six hogsheads of prime Virginia tobacco. The land was destined to remain within the ownership of the Alexander family for the next century although it was allowed to remain dormant, neither cultivated nor inhabited during this period.

George Washington Parke Custis

Martha Dandridge was only 16 at the time of her marriage to Daniel

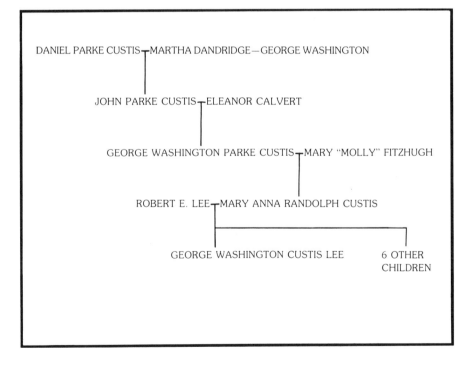

The family tree of the Custis family of Virginia.

Parke Custis, a man 20 years her senior. It was not uncommon in colonial Virginia for women to marry young. As planter William Byrd noted in his diary, "An old maid . . . [is] as scarce among us and reckoned as ominous as a blazing star." For the next 7 years, Daniel and Martha made their home on the Custis plantation located on the Pamunkey River near the colonial capital of Williamsburg. Their marriage produced two off-spring, John Parke and Martha.

Daniel Custis died suddenly in 1757, leaving Martha a young but wealthy widow with two fatherless children. Since death was an unfortunate but ever-present reality in the American colonies, mourning periods were necessarily brief, lasting only a few weeks. Thus, when Martha Custis began a courtship a few months after her husband's demise, few deemed it inappropriate. Indeed, her suitor was an eligible, handsome, young army officer named George Washington who had already seen military action in the French and Indian War. He was now in command of a force of the Virginia state militia defending frontier settlements from attack.

The couple married in 1759 and Washington moved his new family to his Mount Vernon estate located along the western bank of the Potomac River. Once settled, Washington filed papers in the local court to become the legal guardian of both of Martha's children and he provided generously thereafter for their welfare.

The succeeding years were ones of political turmoil in the American colonies as significant economic and philosophical disputes with Great Britain erupted periodically into bloodshed. As the colonies approached independence, George Washington, a well-respected member of the Virginia gentry, served in the House of Burgesses. Later, he was appointed by the Continental Congress to command the colonial army created to oppose the major British forces being sent to America to quell the rebellion.

On the eve of the Revolution, Washington's stepson, John Parke Custis, married Eleanor Calvert and he began to investigate local properties for a possible plantation of his own. In 1778, with Washington's approval, Custis purchased a 1,100-acre estate from Gerald Alexander for 1,100 pounds in Virginia currency. The tract, carved out of the original Howsing land grant, was undeveloped but its wooded lands and excellent location along the Potomac seemed to be ideal for development at the conclusion of the Revolutionary War.

John Custis, at the age of 26, asked his stepfather's permission to enlist in the Continental Army during the crucial campaigns of 1781. Appointed to Washington's personal staff, Custis was at Yorktown in October when the British army was finally cornered by a combined French and American force. He became seriously ill with camp fever during the siege

but despite his frail health, insisted on watching the final surrender ceremonies of the British forces under Lord Cornwallis.

Custis was taken to Eltham to recuperate from his illness. A few weeks
later, his condition deteriorated and his family was summoned to his
bedside. General Washington later recounted, "I arrived [on November
5th] . . . in time to see poor Custis breathe his last." In a subsequent
letter, Washington confided to a friend that, "Mr. Custis' death has given
much distress in this family" and that, "Poor Mrs. Washington . . . has
met with a most severe stroke in the loss of her amiable Son."

John Parke Custis was survived by his wife and two infant children,
George Washington Parke and Nelly. The children were brought to
Mount Vernon to be raised under the guidance of their grandparents.

George Washington Parke Custis, affectionately known to family
members as "Little Washington," was eventually sent to the College of
Philadelphia to complete his formal education. A lackluster student, he
failed to graduate from the institution. He was later enrolled at both
Princeton and Annapolis Colleges without ever completing his studies.
Indeed, George Washington, then serving as President of the new republic, was distressed over his grandson's languid scholarship and was
disheartened to receive a letter from one of Custis' advisors:

> If you . . . could by indirect means discover the state of
> Washington Custis's mind, it would be to be wished. He ap-
> pears to me to be moped and stupid, says nothing, and is
> always in some hole or corner excluded from the company.
> Before he left Annapolis he wrote to me, desiring to know
> whether or not he was to return there. I answered that I was
> astonished at the question, and that it appeared that nothing
> that could be said to him had the least effect. Whether this by
> thwarting his views is the cause of his present behavior I
> know not

To the disappointment of the family, Washington Custis returned to
Mount Vernon in 1798 having failed in his studies and apparently facing
a dismal future. Washington formally wrote to his prodigal grandson an
extensive letter outlining what was expected of him while at the estate,
detailing his hourly and daily responsibilities. Washington went on to
advise "the hours allotted for study, if really applied to it, instead of
running up & down stairs, & wasted in conversation with any one who
will talk with you, will enable you to make considerable progress in
whatsoever line is marked out for you: and that you may do it, is my
sincere wish."

The next year, George Washington died quietly at home and his beloved wife, Martha, followed him in death three years later. Upon his

grandmother's demise, Washington Custis inherited his father's 1,100-acre Potomac plantation which had been held in trust for him. He also inherited many priceless heirlooms from his grandparents' Mount Vernon estate.

Custis began to develop his new land holdings and, in honor of his grandfather, called the property "Mount Washington." Eventually, to avoid confusion with the numerous other "Washingtons" that appeared throughout the states in the aftermath of the first President's demise, the estate was renamed Arlington after the ancestral land holdings of the Custis family on the eastern shore of Virginia.

Washington Custis commissioned the renowned architect, George Hadfield, who had worked on the construction of the United States Capitol, to assist in designing the plantation's manor house. Using the classical-revival style that was popular throughout the United States and dominated the architecture of the nation's capital, the mansion was modeled after the Temple of Theseus in Athens. For financial reasons, the wings

An early view of the nation's capital from Arlington House, 1838.

of the house were constructed first. The entire building process extended over two decades.

Known formally as Arlington House, the mansion was located along the heights that overlooked the burgeoning federal city of Washington, D.C. The Arlington mansion was described in a book published in 1859:

> [Custis] commenced the erection of a beautiful mansion at Arlington, an estate of a thousand acres, left him by his father, and lying upon the west side of the Potomac, opposite Washington city . . . It is a most lovely spot, overlooking the Potomac; and from the noble portico, that adorns its front, so conspicuous from every point of the federal city and its vicinity, he saw that city grow into its present grand proportions, from a humble and uninteresting village.

In 1804, Custis married "Molly" Lee Fitzhugh and the couple soon moved into the newly completed north wing of the Arlington House mansion. Their only child, Mary Anna Randolph, was born there in 1808.

During this period, the Arlington estate was an active farm with the fertile fields closest to the Potomac River used for crops, an orchard, and large grazing areas for the plantation's renowned sheep herds. Early on, Custis began to hold an annual festival, the Arlington Sheep Shearing, which brought local farmers together at the estate to compete in various agriculturally related contests. The highlight of the festivities was an elaborate dinner hosted by Custis at which the local farmers were, "[invited] to dine with him under a range of tents, one of which belonged to the illustrious Washington."

In 1812, Great Britain and the United States once again went to war over the doctrine of freedom of the seas. The American population, however, was deeply divided over the advisability of the war with members of the dwindling Federalist party as vocal opponents to the belligerent policies of President James Madison. Custis, a devout Federalist, likewise was an outspoken critic of the war, claiming that it was ill-advised and unnecessary. Indeed, it was argued that the United States could conceivably lose such a conflict since, at the onset of the hostilities, the nation possessed an infinitesimal standing army comprised of only 6,700 men. Similarly, the nation had a mere 16 naval vessels compared to a mighty British armada of over 600 warships.

In Baltimore, a group of pro-war agitators rioted and attacked the offices of the *Federalist Republican* , a leading opposition newspaper whose editor, Alexander Hanson, had repeatedly denounced the war as "unnecessary, inexpedient." In late July 1812, responding to the assault against the paper, several Revolutionary War veterans, including Generals "Light Horse Harry" Lee [the father of Robert E. Lee] and James McCubbin Lingan, arrived in the city to decry the mob's blatant disregard for the First Amendment and to denounce the war. At a staged rally, Lingan, Lee, and other Federalists were arrested by local militia members for haranguing the gathered crowd. On July 28th, a large mob stormed the jail, taunting the imprisoned Federalists with shouts of "Tory." Furious over the impugning of his patriotism, Lingan stripped off his shirt to reveal an ugly scar he had sustained during the Revolution from a Hessian bayonet and shouted to the crowd, "Does this look like I am a traitor?" His action seemed only to inflame the already hostile mob and Lingan and the other prisoners were repeatedly beaten. The old Revolutionary War general died as a result of the injuries he received.

In an effort to reduce tensions, Lingan's funeral was conducted privately in Georgetown, but the Federalists refused to ignore the martyrdom. (He was subsequently reinterred to Arlington National Cemetery in 1908.) Throughout Washington, poignant eulogies were offered coupled with ample denunciations of the war and President Madison. Washington Custis used the occasion to deliver one of the most eloquent funeral orations; the speech was eventually printed in pamphlet form for wider distribution. Custis was lauded as " . . . possess[ing] the fire of Demosthenes, and his actions the grace of Cicero." His eulogy was said to have made "Old warriors, who had almost forgotten how to weep, [feel] the stream of sympathy stealing down their furrowed cheeks."

In 1814, with the outcome of the war still in doubt, General Robert Ross landed a major force of 4,500 British regulars south of Washington, D.C. Many old Federalists, despite their opposition to the war, volunteered to defend the city from the impending British assault.

Custis manned an artillery battery during the ensuing battle, but the well-trained and heavily armed British force routed the inexperienced Americans. With the remnants of the American militia, Custis was forced to join the humiliating and disorganized retreat. Later that evening, Custis returned in despair to Arlington and watched the British destruction of Washington, including the burning of the proud, new symbols of the republic—the White House and the Capitol.

When the War of 1812 concluded shortly thereafter, the nation once again turned its attention toward domestic problems. The institution of slavery was then seen by most educated Americans as a national, not sectional, problem that had to be jointly resolved. Well-meaning Southerners cooperated with their Northern counterparts in seeking alternative labor sources and a way to abolish the system.

Although he owned 60 slaves, Washington Custis became one of Virginia's leading opponents of slavery, calling it "the mightiest serpent that ever infested the world." Custis even allowed his slaves a limited education and incorporated into his will a provision that required the manumission of all of Arlington's slaves within five years of his death. This mandate was made irrelevant by the onset of the Civil War.

In 1817, the "American Society for Colonizing the Free People of Colour of the United States" was formed to encourage the emancipation of blacks and the subsequent return of the freed men to northern Africa. Custis joined such notables as Henry Clay and John Randolph in supporting the society's efforts; chapters were eventually established in all of the states with the exception of South Carolina. However, even with the modest financial support of the federal government, the American Colonization Society's approach to the insidious institution was impractical and few blacks were ever repatriated.

In 1824, the nation welcomed the return of the Marquis de Lafayette to the United States for a triumphal farewell tour of America. For most Americans, the Marquis remained the embodiment of the ideals of the American Revolution, and his visit was widely celebrated throughout the country with innumerable galas and celebrations held in his honor. In October, Lafayette arrived in Washington, D.C., en route to special ceremonies being conducted in Yorktown for the 43rd anniversary of the British surrender. On the outskirts of Washington, Lafayette was met by an official delegation that included Washington Custis. His carriage was escorted to the center of the city for extensive welcoming ceremonies. After a formal dinner in his honor at the White House hosted by President James Monroe, Lafayette, " . . . paid a private visit to the family of MR. CUSTIS of Arlington." While at the estate, the two distinguished gentlemen freely shared memories of George Washington with Lafayette openly reminiscing about his role in the American Revolution.

Two years later, Custis published a series of articles entitled, "Conversations with Lafayette," which were syndicated in both the *Alexandria Gazette* and the *National Intelligencer* . The articles contained detailed accounts of the Marquis' experiences in the American war for independence and recounted his close, personal friendship with George Washington. During this period, Custis also began to compose modest dramas focusing on historical American events, themes, and settings. Although several of Custis' plays were performed throughout the eastern states and enjoyed moderate popularity, most were undistinguished in terms of literary merit.

Custis was also an amateur painter. His canvases depicted Revolutionary War battle scenes centering around the heroic figure of his grandfather. Six of Custis' paintings are known to exist—the battles of Trenton, Princeton, Germantown, and Monmouth; Washington at Yorktown; and Cornwallis' Surrender at Yorktown.

In 1831, Mary Ann Randolph, the sole offspring of Washington and
Molly Custis, began to receive the attentions of a young Army officer and
recent West Point graduate, Robert E. Lee. Although the Lee lineage was
distinguished, Custis initially did not approve of his daughter's suitor or
courtship. Indeed, the Lee family had suffered a series of well-publicized
and embarrassing financial reversals. The patriarch of the Arlington estate feared that young Lieutenant Lee would be unable to provide adequately for his beloved Mary, reducing her to life on the meager salary of
a lower grade Army officer.

As Lee became a frequent visitor to Arlington, he gradually won the
approval of Washington Custis and on June 30, 1831, Mary Randolph
Custis and Robert E. Lee were married in the drawing room of the Arlington House mansion. The event was tersely noted in the *National Intelligencer*, "Marriage: At Arlington House, by the Rev. Dr. Keith, Lieut.

National Archives

*Members of the U.S. Signal Corps posing next to the graves of Washington and Molly Custis, 1864.
Recent burials of Union soldiers are apparent in the background.*

ROBERT LEE, of the U. States Corps of Engineers, to Miss MARY A. R. CUSTIS, only daughter of G.W.P. CUSTIS, Esq."

The ceremony was marred by a heavy summer rainstorm which delayed the arrival of the minister. Marietta Turner, a member of the wedding party and a Custis relative, later recounted the humorous arrival of the Reverend Keith:

> The night of the wedding at Arlington happened to be one of steady rain, and much fun arose from the appearance of the Reverend Mr. Ruel Keith, who arrived drenched to the skin and though a tall man, was compelled to conduct the nuptial service in the clothes of my cousin, George Washington Parke Custis, a very great gentleman but a very small man so far as inches were concerned.

After a week's repose at Arlington, the newlyweds moved to Lee's duty station at Fort Monroe, Virginia. There the couple made their home for a brief period. As it became apparent that Lee's military career would necessitate prolonged absences from home, it was agreed that Mary should return to Arlington. Over the next several years, six of the seven Lee children were born on the estate.

In 1848, after Lee had returned as a Brevet Colonel from the Mexican War for a brief tour of duty in Washington, Custis was asked to participate in Independence Day ceremonies that would mark the beginning of construction of the Washington Monument. As the last surviving link to the first President, Custis' brief speech honoring his grandfather was an integral part of the festivities. Construction on the 550-foot monument continued unabated until the onset of the Civil War, but the structure was not completed during Custis' lifetime.

In May, 1853 tragedy struck Arlington with the death of Custis' beloved wife, Molly. She was buried in a small plot located in a densely wooded area a short distance from the Arlington House mansion. Deeply distraught over the loss of his wife, Custis survived only for another 4 years and died on October 10, 1857. At his request, the patriarch of the Arlington estate was interred beside his wife. The *National Intelligencer* eulogized:

> It becomes our painful duty to announce the decease of the venerable GEORGE WASHINGTON PARKE CUSTIS, the last of the members of the family of WASHINGTON.
>
> MR. CUSTIS died at Arlington, near this city after a brief illness, on the morning of the 10th instant, in the 77th year of his age . . . Thousands from this country and from foreign lands who have visited Arlington to commune with our de-

parted friend, and look upon the touching memorials there treasured up with care of him who was first in the hearts of his countrymen, will not forget the charm thrown over all by the ease, grace, interest, and vivacity of manners and conversation of him whose voice alas! is silent now. The multitudes of our fellow-citizens accustomed, in the heat of summer, to resort to the shades of Arlington will hereafter miss that old man eloquent, who ever extended to them a warm-hearted welcome and became partaker of their joy.

CHAPTER THREE

Your Old Home Has Been . . . Desecrated

—Robert E. Lee

With the death of his father-in-law in 1857, Colonel Robert E. Lee returned to Arlington and assumed the day-to-day operations of the plantation. In the ensuing years, sectional strife between the North and South intensified, culminating in the secession of seven Southern states in 1861.

Like many Southerners, Lee had dual loyalties—to his state and to his country. He sincerely hoped that his beloved Virginia would remain within the Union despite the election of Abraham Lincoln to the presidency. Such delusions, however, were irrevocably shattered on April 17, 1861, when the Richmond legislature withdrew Virginia's ratification of the United States Constitution, effectively linking the Old Dominion's fate to that of the infant Confederacy. Rather than bear arms against his native state, Lee instead chose to resign his federal commission. He left Arlington on April 22nd to offer his services to the Virginia militia. Later, Lee commented, "a Union that can only be maintained by sword and bayonets . . . has no charm for me." His wife, Mary Custis Lee, remained temporarily behind at Arlington in a futile attempt to maintain normalcy.

Meanwhile, across the Potomac, General Winfield Scott, the elderly commander of the Union Army, recognized the strategic importance of the Arlington plantation. Indeed, Arlington, with its breathtaking view of Washington, could easily have been fortified by the Confederate Army with long and medium-range artillery, thereby placing virtually every federal agency and institution in jeopardy . Rather than allow such an eventuality, Scott ordered federal forces to seize the estate.

On the night of May 23rd in the first major military action of the Civil

Arlington House under Union occupation. The Lee estate was seized by the U.S. Army in May 1861 to prevent Confederate fortification of the plantation's strategic ridges.

War, 14,000 Union troops quietly crossed the Potomac by way of the Long and Aqueduct Bridges (the current sites of the 14th Street and Key Bridges) and occupied Arlington. They simultaneously captured the neighboring port city of Alexandria. This uncontested troop movement was accomplished at the cost of only a single casualty.

With Arlington now firmly under Union occupation, General Irvin McDowell converted the manor house into a headquarters for the Army of the Potomac. P. Regis de Tribriand, a French observer traveling with the Union Army observed: "The tents of the guard and of the servants of the staff were set up in the gardens, trampled by men and animals. The park roads were deeply furrowed by the continual passage of artillery and ammunition wagons everywhere." Radical alterations of the grounds were soon ordered, including the hasty construction of two defensive forts, Whipple and McPherson, as part of the growing defensive perimeter protecting Washington from Confederate attack. Upon hearing of the loss of his property and the subsequent Union actions, in a letter to his daughter Lee lamented, "Your old home has been so desecrated that I cannot bear to think of it. I should have preferred it to have been wiped from this earth, its beautiful hill sunk, and its sacred trees buried rather than have been degraded . . . "

Thousands of Union soldiers converged upon Arlington during the early months of the war. There, inexperienced officers continually drilled and trained the new recruits. In July 1861, General McDowell, pressured by the vocal demands of Northern newspapers for action, prematurely ordered the Army of the Potomac to seize the key railway junction at Manassas, some 20 miles west of the city. A major Confederate force was engaged there. During the ensuing day-long battle, federal forces were routed and forced to retreat in disorder toward Washington. The escaping soldiers were later regrouped only after they reached the relative safety of the new Union fortifications along Arlington Heights.

The disastrous defeat necessitated a change in command. General McDowell was replaced by the young, brash George McClellan who was entrusted with the monumental task of rejuvenating the dispirited Army of the Potomac. McClellan immediately moved into the Arlington House mansion for the winter of 1861-62 and began preparations for the spring campaign season.

In late March 1862, McClellan ferried much of the Army of the Potomac to southeastern Virginia in a bold and daring effort to capture Richmond in a surprise attack from the east. President Lincoln, however, ordered a portion of the Union army to remain behind in the vicinity of the capital, including the defensive fortifications at Arlington, to protect it from a possible Confederate offensive.

Arlington's function as a major Army headquarters was discontinued as the war shifted away from Northern Virginia. Several lower ranking officers moved into the vacant mansion to coordinate the capital's western defenses. Since the war remained relatively distant, many elaborate galas and balls were staged at Arlington House to provide a diversion for the officers. The hundreds of less fortunate enlisted men still stationed in the neighboring forts and camps along Arlington Heights were forced to content themselves with foraging around the Lee estate for materials that would help make their lives more bearable. During this time, the land was denuded of small trees and underbrush while fences were torn down to provide an ample supply of wood for camp fires and rifle pits. The excellent stable facilities at Arlington were used by the cavalry to accommodate their horses and as a staging area for periodic excursions deep into hostile Virginia. Yet the chance for combat remained remote as one Union soldier stationed at Camp Leslie along Arlington Heights lamented in a letter home: "I have not ben so fortuneate to mett any Rebels yet and maby I wont but I sill like soldering."

Arlington House became a major sightseeing attraction for many Washington residents anxious to glimpse the antebellum home of Robert

PENNSYLVANIA

Camp Leslie Dec 9th /61
Arlington hights Vd

Dear Sisters

I take my pen in hand to let you know that I am well and hope that theas few lines will find you the same I have not ben so fortuneate to mett ony Rebels yet and mabey I wont but I sill like soldering but would like to come home to see you all I dont know wen that will be tell Dras that Wash Eli asks me if I here from him and I dont know wat to say I dont know wat I have done to him that he dont wraight to me

A letter from G. McCord who was stationed at Camp Leslie located on Arlington Heights. McCord writes, "I have not ben so fortunate to mett any Rebels."

E. Lee, the now legendary Confederate Commander of the Army of Northern Virginia. President Lincoln made occasional visits to the grounds to escape the burdens of his office and enjoy the solitude of the plantation with its panoramic vista of Washington, D.C.

The Arlington Burial Ground

In 1862, the United States Congress passed "An Act for the Collection of Taxes in the Insurrectionary Districts" which levied property taxes on land claimed by the Confederacy. Under the provisions of the legislation, a tax of $92.07 was assessed on the Arlington plantation. Informed of this situation in 1864, Mrs. Lee, now totally an invalid and confined to a wheelchair, attempted to comply with the law's provisions by sending designated representatives to Union-occupied Alexandria to offer payment. The federal tax commissioners stationed in the city refused to accept the funds on the dubious grounds that the property owners had to appear personally. Shortly thereafter, Arlington was officially confiscated for tax default and the property was sold at auction to the United States government for a mere $26,800.

That same year, the War Department began to assess federal properties as potential burial grounds since the government had received severe criticism for the callous way federal soldiers had been interred in remote and austere locations. Now, with the demand for adequate grave space for the endless stream of Civil War casualties at a peak, Arlington seemed an ideal location for a new federal cemetery with its beautiful setting and large acreage.

On May 13, 1864, a small burial party was ordered to the west bank of the Potomac River near the northeastern boundary of the Lee plantation. There, they interred a hapless new recruit, Private William Christman, 67th Pennsylvania Infantry. Christman, just 21 at the time of his death, had enlisted two months previously and had spent the majority of his brief military career in Lincoln Hospital in a losing battle against peritonitis. His burial on the Lee plantation was near the site of a small cemetery reserved for the plantation's slaves. It was the first military funeral on land that would eventually encompass Arlington National Cemetery.

For the next few weeks, burials continued in this remote section of the Lee estate, but several staff officers stationed on the plantation were opposed to the use of General Lee's estate for burials and argued against any further expansion of grave facilities. Still, the Quartermaster General of the Army, Montgomery Meigs, the individual charged with the administration of federal cemeteries, was angry and embittered over what he perceived to be Lee's treasonable behavior. He requested permission from Secretary of War Edwin Stanton to formally designate 200-acres in the immediate vicinity of the Arlington House mansion as a national cemetery and to encircle the residence with graves thereby making it unsuitable for private habitation. On June 15th, orders were issued to set aside "The Arlington Mansion and the grounds immediately surrounding it . . . for a Military Cemetery. The bodies of all soldiers dying in the Hospitals of the vicinity of Washington and Alexandria . . . will be interred in this Cemetery." The same day that the cemetery was commissioned, 65 burials took place on the property including several in Mrs. Lee's rose garden. By the end of 1864, the graves of over seven thousand Union soldiers located in the "Field of the Dead" (Section 13) scarred the once beautiful landscape and rows of crude wooden markers stretched to the horizon.

The funerals at Arlington were frequently conducted without ceremony or religious services. Quartermaster General Meigs notified the Secretary of War:

> I find that soldiers buried at the military cemeteries in this District are generally interred without any religious ceremony. On inquiry yesterday of the workmen engaged in digging graves where forty soldiers are interred daily, they informed me that they had seldom seen a chaplain at a funeral. Some of them thought none had been there for three weeks. It is impossible for the chaplains of hospitals to accompany each body to the grave. It is a daily duty, and the chaplains' whole time would be taken up in its performance. The Quartermaster's Department is, I think, unjustly blamed for interring the soldiers without appropriate ceremonies. It has not the appointment or employment of chaplains. Its officers are occupied with their appropriate duties, and cannot be present at the cemetery constantly. The interments are going on all day. If from the chaplains attached to the many hospitals of this District one could be detailed daily to be on duty during the whole day at each of the military cemeteries now in use—one at Arlington, the other at Alexandria—it would give great satisfaction to the friends of our soldiers. The chaplain on duty should remain constantly at the cemetery until relieved by his successor. The interments could be made at certain hours two or three times a day, the bodies being deposited at the side of the graves, which are prepared beforehand, and the service could be thus performed over several bodies at a time. If this cannot be done, the only substitute which occurs to me as possible will be the employment by the Quartermaster's Department of an ordained minister at a sufficient salary as a guardian or custodian of each cemetery, making it a part of the contract with him that he shall live at the cemetery in

quarters to be prepared for him, take charge of the whole conduct of interments, and perform appropriate religious services over all persons interred therein. I think that the detail by military authority of a chaplain to this duty daily is the better and more appropriate mode of meeting the difficulty, and I only suggest the employment by the Quartermaster's Department of persons for this purpose as a last resort.

With a cessation of hostilities in 1865, Lee settled in Lexington, Virginia, where he assumed the presidency of Washington College. Mary Lee remained bitter over the loss of her ancestral home and in 1866 wrote to a friend, "I learn that my garden laid out with so much taste by my dear father's own hands has all been changed, the splendid forest levelled to the ground, the small enclosure allotted to his and my mother's remains surrounded closely by the graves of those who aided to bring all this ruin on the children and country. They are even planted up to the very door without any regard to common decency." In a subsequent letter she elab-

National Archives

The Field of the Dead (Section 13). Over 16,000 Union soldiers were buried near the Arlington House mansion to prevent the Lees from ever returning to their antebellum home. These original grave markers were made of wood.

orated, "Even savages would have spared that place . . . yet they have done everything to debase and desecrate it."

Despite the end of battlefield casualties, Arlington's mandate as a national cemetery continued into the post-war period. Cleanup operations were conducted on virtually all major Civil War battlefields since, in the haste of conflict, thousands of soldiers had been left unburied or interred in shallow, inadequate graves which posed a major health problem for the surrounding communities. Near Bull Run, the bones of literally hundreds of soldiers were routinely uncovered and transported to Arlington for burial. A vault was placed in the Lee rose garden to accommodate these remains in a common grave. The *National Intelligencer* graphically described the scene:

> A more terrible spectacle can hardly be conceived than is to be seen within a dozen rods of the Arlington mansion. A circular pit, twenty feet deep and the same in diameter, has been sunk by the side of the flower garden, cemented and divided into compartments, and down into this gloomy receptacle are cast the bones of such soldiers as perished on the field and either were not buried at all or were so covered up as to have their bones mingle indiscriminately together. At the time we looked into this gloomy cavern, a literal Golgotha, there were piled together skulls in one division, legs in another, arms in another, and ribs in another, what were estimated as the bones of two thousand human beings. They were dropping fragmentary skeletons into this receptacle almost daily.

The vault was filled and sealed in September 1866, and a granite monument was placed above it to commemorate the fallen soldiers. The inscription on the sarcophagus reads:

Beneath this stone repose the bones of two
thousand one hundred and eleven unknown soldiers,
gathered after the war from the fields of Bull Run
and the route to the Rappahannock. Their remains could
not be identified, but their names and deaths are
recorded in the archives of their country, and its grateful
citizens honor them as of their noble army of martyrs.
May they rest in peace.

Most Northerners agreed with the government's confiscation of the Lee estate and its conversion to a national cemetery. The *Morning Chronicle* called the creation of the Arlington Burial Ground, "A righteous use of the estate of the rebel General Lee," and charged him with the "[. . .

R. Cramer

The granite sarcophagus erected over the remains of 2,111 unknown soldiers from the Civil War.

murder of] hundreds of Union heroes." Still, a few individuals were distressed over what they perceived to be a vengeful act. One visitor to Arlington after the Civil War wrote:

> We found ourselves at Arlington House looking back across the Potomac at the glorious view of the distant city. The house is placed in a lovely situation on the crest of a beautifully wooded slope. It is a queer old fashion place, with heavy columns and flights of steps, strangely like what it is being now turned into—a mausoleum. In front workmen were busy restoring the outer wall for the park has become enclosed as a cemetery. To see the home of Robert Lee sacked and made into a cemetery, and to fancy the thoughts that would fill the great heart were so strange to me, and in their strangeness so painful, that I doubt whether I ever had a sadder walk than the visit to the heights of Arlington.

Robert E. Lee died in 1870 without ever returning to Arlington. He was buried in the chapel of Washington College which later, in his honor, changed its name to Washington and Lee University. Mary Custis Lee, however, did make one brief and sad pilgrimage to Arlington in 1873 to visit some of her former servants who remained on the estate in the employ of the United States government. Upon arrival, surrounded by the thousands of graves of "enemy" soldiers, Mary Lee was so distraught that she refused to leave her carriage. In utter despair, deprived now of her devoted husband and her beloved Arlington, she returned to Lexington where she lived only another five months.

In accordance with the original will of Washington Custis, claim to Arlington now fell to his eldest grandson and namesake, George Washington Custis Lee. Lee, desirous of claiming his inheritance, asked the United States Congress to recognize his rightful ownership of the Arlington property but they rejected all of his appeals. Advised by his lawyers that his sole recourse was to take legal action, Custis Lee filed suit in the Circuit Court of Alexandria in April 1877 demanding eviction of the federal government from the estate as a trespasser.

The lower court ruled in favor of Lee and ordered the federal government to vacate the property and return it to its antebellum appearance. Faced with the monumental and unpleasant task of disinterring over 16,000 soldiers, the government filed an appeal with the United States Supreme Court in 1882. In *George Washington Custis Lee versus the United States of America* the court, in a five-to-four decision, concurred with the earlier verdict and upheld Lee's claim to Arlington.

Representatives of the government, with all legal recourse exhausted, finally entered into serious negotiations with Custis Lee for the formal purchase of the Arlington estate. Lee agreed to sell the property for $150,000, a fee Congress gladly appropriated in March 1883. Title to the property was officially transferred to the United States on April 24th, forever ensuring Arlington's mandate as a national cemetery.

Post-War Arlington

During the early years of Arlington's existence as a national cemetery, landscaping practices were often primitive and unpredictable. Grave markers were still constructed out of wood and were brutalized by the ravages of time and weather. They required replacement on a regular five-year cycle at a cost to the government of $1.24 each.

Montgomery Meigs, the Quartermaster General charged with the maintenance of federal cemeteries, began to investigate alternative, more enduring grave markers in hopes of reducing government expense. At his order, an experimental stone composed of a metal alloy was placed in Section 13. Although this stone was durable and still remains, the federal government in 1872 adopted the more traditional and aesthetic white marble for use in all national cemeteries. By 1880, rows of new, gleaming

P. Bigler

Wallace Fitz Randolph used a canon as a grave marker. Early cemetery regulations permitted a vast array of funeral architecture causing what some termed "riotous conditions."

white standardized gravestones were evident throughout the Arlington Burial Ground.

Uniform stones were required in enlisted areas, but in Section 1, the Officer's Section, cemetery regulations liberally allowed more decorative stones, limited in size and scope only by a family's personal wealth and imagination. This caused what some described as "riotous conditions." Consequently, a vast array of unique funeral architecture was erected in elaborate efforts to memorialize the lives of the deceased and provide a lasting tribute. Major General Wallace Fitz Randolph, an artilleryman, even had an actual cannon erected over his grave upon his death in 1910. Allegedly, he claimed that he had spent a lifetime behind an artillery piece and preferred to spend an eternity under one.

The grave marker of Lieutenant John Rodgers Meigs, the son of the Quartermaster General and the founder of the cemetery, is also unusual. Lieutenant Meigs served with the Army of the Shenandoah under the command of Philip Sheridan in 1864. In October, near Harrisonburg, Virginia, Meigs carelessly approached three horsemen whom he believed to be civilians. In fact, they were Confederate cavalry wearing rain gear that had partially obscured their uniforms. Meigs, realizing his mistake too late, was mortally wounded in a hail of gunfire.

General Sheridan notified Quartermaster General Meigs of his son's demise and added that the Lieutenant had been killed, "Without resistance of any kind" implying that he had been murdered by Confederate partisans. General Meigs erected a monument to his son showing the young soldier in full military uniform lying prostrate on the ground surrounded by hoofprints, his revolver at his side. The marker remains a pathetic reminder of a tragedy in the Shenandoah Valley a century ago.

Although Arlington was primarily designed for the interment of federal soldiers, many Confederate prisoners of war died in local hospitals and required appropriate military funerals. The cemetery's original burial records show that all such interments were designated with the derogatory term, "REBEL," and indicate that the first Southern soldier buried at Arlington was an unknown Confederate interred on May 20, 1864. Shortly thereafter, on May 30th, the first identifiable Confederate, Levi Reinhardt, 23rd North Carolina Regiment, was buried after his death at Carver Hospital.

After the end of the Civil War, Reinhardt and the remains of many other Southern soldiers were claimed by family members and reinterred to their native states. Those Confederate soldiers who remained at Arlington were often excluded from post-war memorial tributes and denied grave decorations. Only when time had ameliorated the intense passions of the conflict was it decided to pay tribute to the Southern soldiers still buried at Arlington. Not until 1906 did Congress authorize the construction of a Confederate memorial.

The Freedmen's Village

The Freedmen's Bureau under the direction of General O.O. Howard was created in 1865 to look after the welfare of the slaves newly emancipated by the 13th Amendment. A freedmen's village was established on the grounds of the Lee plantation and eventually consisted of over 100 homes housing 1,000 people. The blacks on the estate were taught trades, skills, and reading. *Harper's Weekly* described the village, "[as] quite lively, having a large number of children in it. For these there is a school house; there is, besides, a home for the aged, a hospital, church, tailor and other work-shops, with other public buildings. The principal street is over a quarter of a mile long, and the place presents a clean and prosperous appearance at all times." A contemporary guidebook of Washington, D.C., however, was more critical. It claimed:

> [Arlington Village] is one of the various settlements estab-
> lished by the Government to relieve the Capital from being
> overflowed by the freedmen . . . the village is in the charge of
> the Freedmen's Bureau, and is in better condition than the
> majority of such establishments throughout the country, so
> that it cannot be justly regarded as a fair specimen of them.
> The officers of the Bureau have, frequently, hard work to
> keep the Negroes in subjection, and to enforce their orders.
> Once or twice it has been necessary to summon the aid of the
> military . . . it would seem [appropriate] to abandon it as soon
> as possible, and thus relieve the country of the heavy load of
> taxation which its support renders necessary.

The Freedmen's Bureau was abolished in 1872, but the Arlington Village
remained in existence until the late 1890s when it was finally abolished
because of cemetery expansion.

Arlington is also the final resting place for over 3,800 former slaves.
Most are interred in Section 27 which has traditionally been known as the
"Contraband" section. The term, "contraband," in reference to the run-
away slaves originated with General Benjamin Franklin Butler, the arro-
gant commander of Fort Monroe in Tidewater, Virginia. At the onset of
the Civil War, several slaves fled their plantations and sought refuge
within Fort Monroe. Butler, exceeding this authority and violating stated
administration policy, refused to return the black refugees to their own-
ers claiming that he would, "Hold these Negroes as contraband of war
. . . [since they are] capable of being used for warlike purposes."

Throughout the Civil War, thousands of slaves continually crossed
federal lines and settled in the vicinity of the Union capital of Washington, D.C. Forced to live in cramped quarters with unsanitary conditions,
many of these former slaves died and were buried at Arlington. Their
stones were designated with the inscription, "Civilian," or "Citizen."
Interspersed among these markers are the graves of numerous black soldiers who served in the Union army during the Civil War or with federal
forces in subsequent American conflicts before integration of the Armed
Forces. Their graves bear the abbreviation U.S.C.T for United States Colored Troops.

The First Memorial Day

In 1868, as Arlington's size swelled with the continuing burial of Civil
War veterans, General John Alexander Logan issued General Order #11
which created Decoration Day, a time for the nation to honor deceased
veterans. The order read in part:

> The 30th day of May, 1868, is designated for the purpose of

strewing with flowers, or otherwise decorating the graves of comrades who died in defense of their country during the late rebellion . . . We should guard their graves with sacred vigilance . . . Let no neglect, no ravages of time, testify to the present or to the coming generations that we have forgotten as a people the cost of a free and undivided republic . . . Let us, then, at the time appointed, gather around their sacred remains, and garland the passionless mounds above them with the choicest flowers of springtime; let us raise above them the dear old flag they saved; let us in this solemn presence renew our pledge to aid and to assist those whom have left among us a sacred charge upon the Nation's gratitude— the soldier's and sailor's widow and orphan.

In keeping with the spirit of Logan's order, the first commemorative celebrations were conducted at Arlington House and attended by Generals Grant and Garfield, both future presidents. A contemporary account in the *New York Times* described the festivities:

The ceremonies consequent upon the decoration of the soldiers' graves at the Arlington National Cemetery were most imposing and impressive. About 10:30 o'clock the Committee completed their labors, and four large army wagons were filled with evergreens of every description, and the Committee of Arrangements, accompanied by the ladies who assisted in preparing the flowers, proceeded to Arlington Heights in carriages, omnibuses and ambulances, via the Long Bridge. Upon their arrival at Arlington, the flowers and evergreens were turned over to the Decoration Committee, who took charge of them until the time arrived for the decoration of the grounds. About the same hour throngs of people, in every manner of vehicle, from gorgeous private equipages, with liveried coachmen and outriders, and public carriages to the more modest rockaways of humble citizens, started for the grounds. Some idea of the immense crowd may be formed from the fact that more than three hundred vehicles passed the Arlington toll gate en route to the cemetery, and it is estimated that at least five thousand pedestrians were present. The day was propitious, although somewhat too warm for comfort, but nevertheless the prearranged program was carried out without variation.

GEN. GARFIELD, of Ohio, delivered the address . . . The most impressive feature in the ceremonies was the procession of the children of the Soldiers' and Sailors' Orphan Asylum, in charge of the officers and managers of the Association, and Committee on Decorations, followed by friends generally. As the procession moved around the garden south of the mansion, the children strewed flowers upon the graves along the line of march, and halted at the tomb of the unknown soldiers who fell in Virginia from Bull Run to the Rappahannock during the early years of the war. The monument contains an inscription appropriate to their valor, and states that the dust of 2,111 soldiers is there commingled. The children, boys and girls, wearing mourning scarfs, sung a plaintive song, and during the playing of the Dead March by the Fifty Cavalry Band, the tomb was appropriately decorated amid marked solemnity, many shedding tears. Meantime a national salute was fired from the front of the Arlington House. The procession then re-formed and marched to the flag stand at the principal cemetery. There was a prayer, a hymn by eight male voices, and the reading of President LINCOLN'S dedicatory address at Gettysburg, the last named by HON. HALBERT E. PAINE, of Wisconsin, a General in the late war. The Committee on Decorations, with the orphans, then deployed and took positions at the different stands of flowers and flags, and at once proceeded to the decoration of the graves throughout the Cemetery. The bands relieved each other in playing appropriate music. The ceremonies concluded with the air of the Star-Spangled Banner, a prayer and benediction.

The popularity of the holiday increased in ensuing years and was finally declared a national holiday by act of Congress in 1888 and renamed Memorial Day. The crowds for subsequent Memorial Day services at Arlington grew so large that the limited facilities at the mansion were inadequate to accommodate all who wished to participate. Congress appropriated funds for the construction of an amphitheater to be located just south of Arlington House near the monument to the 2,111 unknown soldiers. Its planned size would be capable of accommodating up to 1,500 people. The trellised structure, completed in 1874, was described in a turn of the century guidebook: "Here art and nature have joined hands and formed one of those delightful combinations which touch the heart, and upon the hallowing velvet turf the companies who have come here upon Memorial Day have their patriotism quickened by the recital of the valorous deeds of those who died."

Civil War Notables

Among the Civil War notables buried at Arlington, Philip Kearny was one of the most interesting. Despite failing to graduate from West Point, Kearny nonetheless was commissioned and saw action in the war with Mexico. In a daring and chivalrous cavalry charge at Churubusco, he lost an arm but won the adulation of the American commander, Winfield Scott, who called Kearny, "The bravest man I ever saw, a perfect soldier."

Kearny continued his military career after the war and sought action in Europe where he joined the French in their campaigns in Algiers. He received the French Grand Cross for bravery for his actions in northern Africa. He later returned to the United States where he received a command in the newly formed Army of the Potomac. He earned the respect of his men by creating the famed "Kearny Patch," a diamond- shaped insignia which was worn by his troops on their kepis and proudly distinguished them as members of "Fighting Phil's Red Diamond Regiment."

In 1862, after the disastrous battle of Second Bull Run, Kearny's men engaged a major Confederate force near Chantilly, Virginia. As night approached and both lines became confused, he rode into a Confederate position. Ignoring shouts to surrender, Kearny instead wheeled his horse around and attempted to escape in a hail of gunfire. Several bullets struck the General killing him instantly. His body was taken behind the Confederate lines to the headquarters of a former West Point classmate, General A.P. Hill. Hill sadly gazed upon his friend's body and lamented, "Poor Kearny, he deserved a better death than that."

When General Robert E. Lee was notified of Kearny's demise, he immediately ordered the body to be returned to the Union lines under a flag of truce. Likewise, all of Kearny's possessions, including his horse, were similarly returned. Lee later compensated the Confederate government for these captured items out of his own personal funds.

Kearny was buried near the Old Amphitheater at Arlington Cemetery, his grave marked by one of the cemetery's two equestrian statues, a gift from the state of New Jersey in 1914.

Nearby is the grave of James Tanner, a little known corporal who played a major role in American history. Tanner enlisted in the Union Army at the age of 19 and was seriously wounded during the second battle of Manassas in 1862. Surgeons were forced to amputate both of his legs, but Tanner was later able to walk after being fitted with two wooden prostheses. Unable to contribute further to the Union cause as a soldier, Tanner studied stenography, a vital skill in the era of handwritten records and eventually found employment with the War Department in Washington.

On the evening of April 14, 1865, Tanner attended a gala at Grover's Theater in Washington, D.C., celebrating Lee's surrender of the Army of Northern Virginia. Midway through the festivities, word was received that President Abraham Lincoln had been shot across town at Ford's Theater. Tanner, initially believing that the report was false, attempted to calm the panicked crowd. When the rumor was confirmed, Tanner, along with many of the other theatergoers, hurriedly made their way to 10th Street, the site of the shooting.

The President's limp body had been carried across the street from Ford's Theater to the Peterson boarding house. His attending physicians did not believe the President could survive even a short trip back to the White House. Around midnight, Tanner volunteered to record the testimony of the witnesses to the shooting. Throughout the remainder of the night, sitting opposite Secretary of War Edwin Stanton, Tanner took copious shorthand notes as the pursuit of the assassins was planned and organized. He later recalled that, "In fifteen minutes I had enough down to hang John Wilkes Booth." Tanner's record of the events at the Peterson boarding house remains the most comprehensive and accurate account of the hours immediately after the Lincoln assassination.

General Arthur MacArthur, father of General of the Army Douglas MacArthur, is buried a few yards from Tanner. He served with the 24th Wisconsin during the Civil War and had a renowned military career. He received the Congressional Medal of Honor for his actions in 1863 during the Battle of Missionary Ridge when he led his troops in a valiant charge against a strongly fortified Confederate position maintained by the Army of the Tennessee. The Union victory, resulting in part from this action, opened the way for Sherman's invasion of Georgia and the famed march to the sea which doomed the Confederate cause.

Eighty years later, MacArthur's son, Douglas, would likewise be awarded the Congressional Medal of Honor for his heroic defense of the Philippines during the Japanese assault on the islands in 1941-42. Together, they remain the only father and son recipients of the nation's highest decoration of valor.

In Section 1, the grave of the legendary founder of the game of baseball, Abner Doubleday, can be found. He graduated from West Point and became an officer in the Civil War like many other graduates. He was with the Union garrison at Fort Sumter, South Carolina in April 1861 and fired the first federal response to Confederate cannonade during the event that marked the beginning of hostilities in the Civil War.

Doubleday later served in most of the major campaigns in the eastern theater of operations, fighting in the battles of Manassas, Antietam, Fredericksburg, and Gettysburg. At Gettysburg, Doubleday assumed command of General Reynold's regiment after the commander was killed. Under Doubleday's leadership, two Confederate brigades were virtually annihilated and his troops helped repel Pickett's charge on the last, crucial day of the battle.

Despite such valor and notable service, Doubleday is most remembered for something he neither did nor claimed—the founding of baseball. Several years after his death, a commission was created in 1907 to investigate the origins of the national pastime. Headed by Albert Spalding, the commission reported that, "Baseball had its origin in the United States [and that it] was devised by Abner Doubleday at Cooperstown, New York in 1839."

Doubleday's name and the city of Cooperstown, the home of baseball's Hall of Fame, became forever linked to the game despite historical evidence that clearly refuted the Spalding committee's findings. Indeed, Doubleday was not even in Cooperstown during 1839 and in his copious writings, which include thousands of pages of diaries, letters, and speeches, there is not the slightest mention of baseball. Still, the myth remains strong and, to most Americans, Abner Doubleday continues to be the "Father of Baseball."

The burial of such notable figures as Doubleday, Tanner, and MacArthur enhanced Arlington's new identity as a national cemetery. By the end of the 19th century, it had become the most widely known of the national cemeteries. It truly reflected the spirit of Theodore O'Hara's poem whose verses were strategically placed on bronze plaques through the cemetery:

> On fame's eternal camping ground
> Their silent tents are spread
> And glory guards with solemn round
> The bivouac of the dead.

CHAPTER FOUR

Where Valor
Proudly Sleeps

—Theodore O'Hara

In 1886, John Commerford, a partially disabled Civil War veteran, was appointed superintendent of Arlington National Cemetery. He moved into the Lee mansion which had been converted into a residence for the cemetery's chief administrator. Commerford was enthusiastically described in an early inspection report as, "intelligent, well-educated, energetic, and capable." The report went on to declare, "the general condition of the cemetery was good," but also warned that, "Being in the vicinity, there are, in spite of the difficulty in getting there, many visitors, many of them rough characters."

The greatest problem facing Commerford in the late 19th century was cemetery expansion. Arlington's original 200 acres now contained the remains of over 19,000 soldiers and servicemen. These numbers were being augmented by slightly over 300 interments annually. The cemetery would shortly be unable to accommodate any further burials without a major acquisition of new acreage. The logical area for expansion was westward toward the Freedmen's Village which continued to operate within the confines of the original Lee estate.

After the government's settlement with Custis Lee in 1883, all doubt concerning the ownership of Arlington had been removed. Legally, the former Lee estate was an Army reservation subject to government regulations which technically prohibited civilians from residing on a military post.

On November 12, 1887, Superintendent Commerford directed a letter to the Deputy Quartermaster General of the Army requesting the eviction of black residents from the premises claiming that the inhabitants were frequently trespassing on the cemetery grounds and pilfering firewood:

> I would respectfully report that for years past some of the colored people who live on the reservation have been in the habit of entering the cemetery during the late hours of the night for the purpose of getting wood for fuel.
> On my arrival here, one year ago, I was informed that several hundred young forest trees, from 2 to 6 inches in diameter were cut down and carried away. The remains of those trees can yet be seen.
> It has been the custom of these thieves, to use a cross cut saw to cut down trees. By so doing, very little noise is made, in order to avoid detection. It is said, that very few of these squatters buy any fuel, and depend mostly on what they can pick up within the enclosure. It would be necessary for a man to remain on watch all night, to arrest the guilty parties. It has been suggested, that the most effective way of preventing such thefts, is to cause the removal of these people from the reservation.

The Quartermaster General's office quickly responded:

> In Violation of paragraph #138 Army Regulations, amended by General Order #26, Adjutant General's Office, 1883, civilians are residing upon the Military reservation, upon which the Arlington National Cemetery and the Military Post at Fort Myer, Va., are located.
> This occupation has continued many years, and since the title of the land passed to the United States by purchase, May 18, 1883, no steps have been taken for the removal of these occupants, mostly colored people.
> In consequence of the complaints now made, it would seem to be proper that they should be ordered to vacate their holdings, giving them sufficient time for moving their property to prevent suffering.
> I therefore recommend that the Military Authorities at Fort Myer be directed to serve notice upon all Civilians residing on the reservation, and not employed by the Government, that they must remove therefrom, within 90 days after date of notice.

Over the next few years, the Freedmen's Village slowly disappeared. The cemetery gained 142 acres in 1889 and an additional 56 acres in 1897. By the turn of the century, Arlington had become the largest of the 83 national cemeteries.

Federal law required Arlington and all national cemeteries to enclose the grounds with a fence. Arlington used this government mandate to construct three impressive entry gates to the cemetery, memorializing four major Civil War generals—Sheridan, Ord, Weitzel, and McClellan.

The cemetery's main entrance was named for General Philip Sheridan who was buried at Arlington in 1888. He was the Union cavalry commander who relentlessly pursued Confederate troops through the Shenandoah Valley during the brutal campaigns of 1864. The gate consisted of four stately white columns which had been removed from the old War Department building in Washington before its demolition in 1879. Each pillar was individually inscribed with the name of an additional Civil War figure—Scott, Lincoln, Stanton, and Grant. The large iron gates bore the Latin phrase, "It is sweet and glorious to die for the Fatherland."

Entrance to the lower cemetery, the site of the earliest burials at Arlington, was through the Ord-Weitzel gate, named for Major Generals Edward Ord and Godfrey Weitzel, Union officers during the Civil War. Ord had been a major figure in the capture of Jackson, Mississippi, and was present during the siege of Petersburg. Weitzel was one of the Union Army's most experienced engineers and officer-in-charge of the 1865 occupation forces in Richmond. The gate consisted of twin white pillars, also taken from the old War Department building. After a major land acquisition and the resulting expansion of the cemetery eastward in the late 1960s, the gates were rendered useless and were finally torn down.

The only surviving original gate was named for General George McClellan, the "Young Napoleon," who made his headquarters temporarily at Arlington while in command of federal forces. The large, red sandstone edifice became a model for similar gates in national cemeteries located in Chattanooga, Nashville, and Vicksburg. The McClellan gate is no longer functional but has been retained for its historical significance. Inscribed above the archway are the cemetery's Civil War statistics: "Here rests 15,585 of the 315,555 Citizens who Died in the Defense of our Country from 1861 to 1865." A portion of Theodore O'Hara's poem appears on the structure as well: "Rest on Embalmed and Sainted Dead, Dear as the Blood ye Gave and Glory Guards with Solemn Round the Bivouac of the Dead." Of the various individuals commemorated by the three gates, only Generals Sheridan and Ord are actually interred at Arlington Cemetery.

In 1892, in an effort to make Arlington cemetery representative of all the nation's wars, four Revolutionary War soldiers—Generals Thomas Meason and James House, Paymaster General Caleb Swan, and LTC William Burrows—were reinterred from their original resting place at the Old Presbyterian Cemetery in Georgetown to Section 1. In addition, fourteen unknowns from the War of 1812 were also buried at Arlington in 1905 after their remains were recovered during a renovation of the Washington Barracks. They were apparent victims of the British assault and burning of the city a century earlier.

The most celebrated figure reinterred during the early 20th century was Major Pierre L'Enfant. L'Enfant, a French national who emigrated to the United States in 1777, served with the Continental Army in the engineering corps during the American Revolution. After the war and the subsequent adoption of the United States Constitution, Congress authorized the construction of a new capital. The city was to be located in the South in, "a district of territory not exceeding ten miles square . . . on the river Potomac for the permanent seat of Government of the United States." It was literally to be a city out of the wilderness, completely designed and planned to emphasize the infant nation's republican ideals and was to be completed by December 1800.

Pierre L'Enfant, a skilled and talented draftsman, was commissioned to diagram the layout and to create a metropolis, "magnificent enough to grace a great nation." L'Enfant, a temperamental and difficult man, was ultimately dismissed. Major alterations were subsequently made to his blueprints and these were implemented in the development of the federal city. Angry and embittered, L'Enfant continually petitioned Congress for payment for his services and drafts but was unsuccessful in recouping adequate payment. He received only $2,394 for his labor and died virtually penniless in 1825. He was buried in obscurity on the Digges Farm in Prince George's County, Maryland. Decades later, Congress finally decided to recognize L'Enfant's contributions to the development of the District of Columbia and, in 1909, L'Enfant's remains were exhumed and brought to the United States Capitol to lie in state in the Rotunda, resting upon the Lincoln catafalque. On April 28th, after a series of tributes and memorial services, his body was taken to Arlington National Cemetery and buried in a prominent location in front of the Arlington House mansion on a hill overlooking the city he envisioned. His monument, designed by W.W. Bosworth, bears an engraving of one of L'Enfant's early maps of the District of Columbia.

The Confederate Memorial

In 1906, Congress authorized the construction of a Confederate memorial. Moses Ezekiel, a Southern veteran of the Battle of New Market and a renowned sculptor, was commissioned to design the monument. On June 4, 1914, the birthday of Jefferson Davis, the Confederate Memorial was formally dedicated with President Woodrow Wilson delivering the principal address.

The monument's central feature is a bronze female figure representing

R. Cramer

The Confederate Memorial. The monument commemorates the 409 Southern soldiers buried at Arlington.

the South in peace. Facing in the direction of the former Confederacy, she holds a plow stock symbolically referring to the Biblical passage from the book of Isaiah, "They shall beat their swords into plow shares." The principal inscription pays tribute to all Southern soldiers and reads:

> Not for fame or reward
> Not for place or for rank
> Not lured by ambition
> Or goaded by necessity
> But in simple
> Obedience to duty
> As they understood it
> These men suffered all
> Sacrificed all
> Dared all — and died.

All 409 Confederate soldiers buried at Arlington were reinterred to Jackson Circle and buried around the base of the memorial. The South ern gravestones, however, are slightly different from their Union counterparts, coming to a point at the top. Legend maintains that these pointed stones were originally designed to keep Yankees from sitting on the graves of their former opponents.

Spanish-American War

War once again came to the United States in 1898 placing additional demands on Arlington. By the end of the 19th century, the Spanish empire in North America had been reduced to Cuba and a few, small Caribbean islands. Local insurgents, dissatisfied with decades of harsh colonial rule, had begun to rebel, prompting a strong and brutal Spanish reaction.

On January 25, 1898, as the Caribbean region became more destabilized, President William McKinley ordered the battleship *U.S.S. Maine* to Havana, Cuba, ostensibly to protect American citizens and property but simultaneously to demonstrate the power and might of the United States Navy.

On the night of February 15th, while peacefully docked in the harbor, a powerful explosion occurred on the *Maine* and the ship rapidly sank killing 260 members of the crew. The jingoistic press in the United States demanded immediate military action and increased popular outrage against Spain with such inflammatory slogans as, "Remember the *Maine* and to hell with Spain." An American investigation into the sinking was ordered by the President to determine culpability in the explosion. After several weeks of inquiry, the commission concluded that the *Maine* had been sunk by a submarine mine and placed blame squarely on the Spanish government.

With public opinion now demanding retaliation for the sinking, McKinley asked Congress for a declaration of war against Spain on April 11, 1898. For the next year, the United States fought what was popularly termed, "A splendid little war," marked by numerous military victories and major territorial acquisition.

The United States military sustained only 385 combat-related fatalities during the Spanish-American conflict, but an additional 2,000 servicemen died from various tropical diseases and illnesses. Many remains of these soldiers and sailors were returned from foreign battlefields and stations for burial at Arlington Cemetery in accordance with an 1899 presidential proclamation which stated: " . . . the remains . . . of the brave officers and men who perished, there has been reserved interment in ground sacred to the soldiers and sailors . . . at the National Cemetery at Arlington."

The burial of the Spanish-American War soldiers at Arlington represented the first time in our history that American servicemen who served abroad in a foreign war were repatriated to the United States for reinterment. The National Society of Colonial Dames in 1902 erected a monu-

The battleship Maine *entering Havana harbor. Two weeks later the ship exploded, killing 260 members of the crew.*

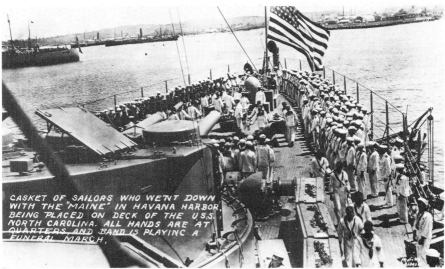

The Maine *dead being returned to the United States for burial at Arlington National Cemetery.*

ment in Section 22 to honor, " . . . the soldiers and sailors of the United States who gave their lives for their country in the war of 1898-99 with Spain."

The victims of the *Maine* tragedy, the *casus belli* of the conflict, were buried initially in Havana, Cuba, in the Colon Cemetery. The catastrophic nature of their deaths, however, made identification difficult; only 63 of the 160 recovered bodies could actually be identified. Fighting on the island in 1898 between American and Spanish forces delayed plans for the return of the *Maine* crew to the United States for appropriate burial.

In the following year, the Navy exhumed 151 of the sailors from the Cuban cemetery. Funeral arrangements were complicated because most of the remains had commingled, having been initially interred six to a grave. The Navy, therefore, rejected the requests of family members for private interments and insisted instead on burying the dead together as a crew on Hall's Knoll at Arlington National Cemetery. The 150 flag-draped coffins were transported back to the United States on board the battleship, *Texas* , the sister ship of the *Maine* , now commanded by the sunken vessel's surviving commanding officer, Captain Sigsbee.

On December 27, 1899, the coffins were transported to Arlington on wagons to await burial scheduled for the following day. The remains were placed under tents with a detachment of Marines deployed to guard them. At 11 o'clock on the morning of the 28th, funeral services began despite an untimely Washington snowfall. President William McKinley led the mourners who included the two major naval heroes of the Spanish-American War, Captain Sigsbee and Admiral Dewey.

Individual wreaths were placed upon each coffin during the services which concluded with the playing of "Taps." The ceremonies, however, were marred by the presence of aggressive cameramen, eager to photograph the rows of flag-draped coffins lying in open trenches. The *Washington Evening Star* recounted:

> There were seemingly a score of [photographers], in fact, and during the solemn service they made themselves most obnoxious by snapping pictures from every point of view. While the chaplains were praying the camera men were rushing about, setting their machines here and there. Finally several of them actually got between the chaplains and the graves and there snapped their kodaks. They seemed to have absolutely no regard for the meaning and solemnity of the occasion. A large sign posted by the cemetery authorities to the effect that no pictures shall be made of funeral services at Arlington was evidently disregarded. Once the photographers were within the grounds to have stopped them in their

sacrilegious intrusion would have necessitated an interruption of the ceremonies, and this was not at all desirable.

The *Maine* , itself, remained submerged in Havana harbor until 1910 when the United States Congress appropriated funds for its salvage, primarily to recover the remaining bodies of the 66 sailors still entombed on the ship and eventually to provide "for proper interment of the bodies . . . in Arlington Cemetery." After Naval recovery efforts had retrieved the bodies of the crew, the ship's mast was removed before the *Maine* was towed out to sea and scuttled. Only one of the recovered bodies from the ship could positively be identified and his remains were returned to family members for private interment. The other 65 sailors were unknown, and they were jointly buried at Arlington Cemetery alongside their compatriots.

A memorial to the *Maine* dead was dedicated on February 15, 1915, the 17th anniversary of the ship's sinking. It is situated adjacent to the graves of the sailors who had served on the vessel. The focal point of the monument is the *Maine* 's mast which is mounted on a simulated battleship gun turret. The names of all 260 casualties of the ship's explosion have been inscribed on the base.

Early Aviation

During the period following the Spanish-American War, the United States Army began efforts to modernize. Experiments by the Wright brothers with a heavier than air flying machine had drawn particular interest from the Army which saw the invention as potentially useful in the airborne observation of hostile troops. Thus, the United States Signal Corps challenged possible developers to test their aircraft before a panel of military observers at Fort Myer, Virginia, adjacent to Arlington Cemetery. The Signal Corps specifications required that a suitable plane must be capable of carrying a minimum of two passengers at 40 miles per hour for at least 60 minutes of sustained flight. Supremely confident, Orville Wright brought a prototype airplane to Arlington for the trials scheduled for the fall of 1908.

The spectacle of manned flight drew large crowds to the military post, including such notables as Secretary of War and presidential hopeful, William Howard Taft. For the next several days, Wright gave repeated successful demonstrations before the panel of observers. However, on September 17th, a young Army lieutenant, Thomas Selfridge, volunteered to be a passenger on one of Wright's test flights. Shortly after takeoff, one of the propellers split and the plane lost control, plummeting to the ground near the western wall of Arlington Cemetery. Wright was seriously injured in the crash and Selfridge, despite immediate medical attention, died a few hours later at Walter Reed Medical Hospital from the injuries he sustained. Selfridge was buried with full military honors at Arlington National Cemetery, the first casualty of modern aviation. In his honor, the western gate to the cemetery near the original crash site was renamed the Selfridge Gate.

The Memorial Amphitheater

In 1914, the major European powers went to war. President Woodrow Wilson steadfastly proclaimed American neutrality in the conflict and the nation attempted to ignore the crisis.

On October 13th of the following year, ceremonies were conducted at Arlington National Cemetery to mark the beginning of construction of a new Memorial Amphitheater. The building, authorized by Congress in 1913, was designed to accommodate Memorial Day crowds of up to 5,000 people and provide a place for other commemorative services.

The theme for the services was, "Lest We Forget." The principal address was delivered by the Secretary of the Navy, Josephus Daniels. Daniels reminded the assembled crowd of the substantial role Arlington played in United States history: "Perpetual be the national spirit that brings annually on a pilgrimage to this spot the national consciousness and the national conscience. Here is the heart of the Republic." He went on to explain the noble goals of all the nation's wars in which many of Arlington's dead had fought:

> It is a good thing to recognize the character of our wars. Our wars against the Indians were not wars of hatred, but they were to protect life and extend and teach civilization. The revolution was for liberty. The war of 1812 was for liberty on sea as well as on land. The Mexican war was to protect our borders. Our civil war was the chastening of a nation to make it see its destiny when it would not . . . The Spanish war gave liberty to millions and guaranteed republics for all portions of the American hemisphere. All the wars which we have ever waged were to get liberty for ourselves or to give it to others. Life is not so sweet as liberty.

A 35-star Civil War flag was flown at half-staff throughout the opening ceremonies on a flag pole specially erected for the occasion. President Woodrow Wilson laid the cornerstone to the Amphitheater. It contained designs for the structure, an autographed photo of the President, and a copy of the day's program along with various other memorabilia from the period. Once the stone was in place, the Civil War flag was replaced with a new, 48-star banner, symbolizing the recent completion of Ameri-

National Archives

The dedication ceremonies of the Memorial Amphitheater.

can continental expansion. President Wilson's participation in the Amphitheater ceremonies established the precedent for presidential visits to the building, a tradition that has been continued by all of his successors during their tenures as chief executive.

The years after 1914 saw an increase in tension between the United States and the European belligerents. The sinking of the *Lusitania* combined with reports of German atrocities in neutral Belgium, enraged the American population. Still, in the 1916 presidential campaign, Wilson adopted the slogan, "He Kept Us out of War." During Memorial Day services at the Old Amphitheater that same year, however, Wilson used the occasion to urge all American young men to volunteer for military service and warned Germany that the United States was prepared, "to become partners in any alliance of nations that would guarantee public right above selfish aggression."

In 1917, after the Germans initiated a policy of unlimited submarine warfare, several American ships were sunk in international waters by patrolling U-boats. The United States Congress adopted a declaration of war and, for the first time in the nation's history, American combat troops were sent to liberate Europe. Wilson again used his traditional Arlington Memorial Day address for a major foreign policy statement by outlining the noble goals for the United States' entry into World War I: "We did not set this government up in order that we might have a selfish

Aerial view of the newly completed Memorial Amphitheater, 1920. The Tomb of the Unknown Soldier was not added until the following year. The Confederate Memorial and the Mast of the Maine memorial are visible in the background.

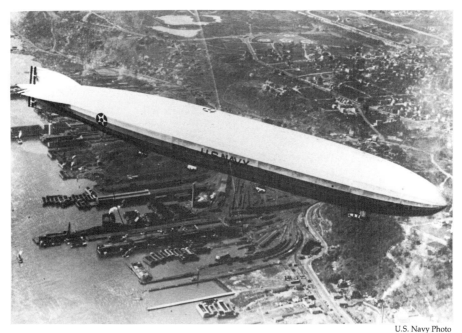

U.S. Navy Photo

The dirigible Shenandoah *in flight over New Jersey. The airship crashed during a violent thunderstorm in 1925 killing 14 Navy aviators.*

and separate liberty, for we are now ready to come to [Europe's] assistance and fight out upon the fields of the world the cause of human liberty."

The injection of fresh American troops into the conflict was sufficient to break the stalemate within a year and on November 11, 1918, an armistice was declared and the war was brought to a successful conclusion. The United States lost 116,708 soldiers in the war, most of whom were initially buried in France until arrangements could be made for the return of their remains to the United States. In the years following the war, a constant stream of American war dead were consigned to new graves at Arlington.

The war slowed the construction of the Memorial Amphitheater and it was not completed until 1920. Dedication ceremonies for America's "Temple of Patriotism" were held on May 15th of that year and were attended by surviving veterans of the Civil War, Spanish-American War, and World War I. President Wilson, still partially paralyzed by a stroke, was unable to attend the services but did send a wreath to mark the auspicious occasion.

The Memorial Amphitheater continues to commemorate American military leaders and great battles from the Revolution through the Spanish-American War. Over the stage area are words from George Washington: "When we assumed the soldier we did not lay aside the citizen." A portion of Lincoln's Gettysburg Address is also inscribed on the Amphitheater: "We here highly resolve that these dead shall not have died in vain."

The Amphitheater was originally constructed with 48 crypts located under the colonnade. These were intended to accommodate the remains of "favorite sons" of individual states, but the subsequent expansion of the nation and the difficulty in establishing adequate protocol forced abandonment of the project. Many of the crypts were demolished during renovation of the building in 1976 to create office space and new restroom facilities. Existing crypts, popularly known as the "catacombs," are used for storage and for drill practice by members of the Tomb guard during off-duty days.

The *Shenandoah*

Although the airplane played only a minor role in the outcome of World War I, some visionaries, including General Billy Mitchell, saw the need for an expanded role of aviation in the military. Indeed, Mitchell argued that aircraft could be a potentially decisive weapon.

Mitchell's appeal for an air force suffered a serious setback on September 3, 1925, when the dirigible *Shenandoah* crashed in Ohio during a violent thunderstorm. Fourteen Naval aviators died including Mitchell's close friend, Lieutenant Commander Zachary Landsdowne, the commander of the vessel.

Landsdowne and three of his fellow officers were brought to Arlington National Cemetery for funeral services. The four aviation pioneers were interred near the grave of three-time unsuccessful presidential candidate, William Jennings Bryan, just off Dewey Circle.

Robert Todd Lincoln

On a shaded hill at the cemetery overlooking the Lincoln Memorial is the grave of Robert Todd Lincoln, the son of President Abraham Lincoln. He was Lincoln's eldest child, born in 1843. His three brothers, Eddie, Willie, and Tad, all died before reaching maturity, leaving Robert to continue the Lincoln legacy.

During the Civil War, Robert witnessed his father's greatest crisis at a distance while attending Harvard College. Upon graduation in January 1865, he requested permission to enlist in the Union Army as a private but the President, having already buried two of his children, was reluctant to risk the life of a third in a war that was nearly won. Lincoln wrote to General-in-Chief U.S. Grant, "My son, now in his 22nd year, having graduated at Harvard, wishes to see something of the war before it ends. I do not wish him put in the ranks, nor yet to give him a commission, to which those who have already served long, are better entitled, and better qualified to hold." Grant responded by making Robert a captain on his personal staff, a position that allowed the young Lincoln to witness Lee's surrender at Appomatox Courthouse. On April 14, 1865 he recounted the dramatic scene to his father at the White House but declined an invitation at the same time to attend an evening performance of Laura Keene in "Our American Cousin" at Ford's Theater.

At the theater that evening, President Lincoln was mortally wounded by an assassin. Robert, informed of the shooting while at the White House, hurried to the President's deathbed at the Peterson boarding house. There, he tried in vain to comfort his grieving and hysterical mother, Mary Todd, while the President slowly succumbed to the bullet wound.

Mary Todd Lincoln never recovered from her husband's assassination and wore mourning garb for the remainder of her life. Having suffered through the loss of two children from disease and the deaths of three brothers in combat during the Civil War on the side of the Confederacy, the death of her youngest son, Tad, in 1871 finally caused her to go insane. Robert Lincoln, the sole heir, was forced to sign the commitment papers to confine his mother to a sanitarium. Discharged five years later, Mary Todd vehemently denounced Robert and his wife, Mary Harlan, and claimed preposterously that they coveted her inheritance.

In 1881, President James Garfield appointed Robert Todd Lincoln to his cabinet as Secretary of War. Lincoln escorted the President to the Baltimore and Potomac Railroad Station (the site of the National Gallery of Art) on July 2 of that year where the President was to embark on a vacation to the New Jersey shore. Instead, Robert was witness to Garfield's assassination by Charles Guiteau, a frustrated and mentally deranged office seeker. Two decades later, on September 6, 1901, Lincoln was attending the Pan-American Exposition in Buffalo, New York, and was present when President William McKinley was assassinated, thereby becoming the only person to be present at the deaths of the three assassinated American presidents.

Robert Lincoln's auspicious political career also included an appointment as the United States Minister to Great Britain under the Benjamin Harrison administration. Lincoln's wife, Mary Harlan, and their son, Abraham "Jack" Lincoln II, accompanied him to his post in London. Jack was soon sent to school in Versailles, France, to study the language in preparation for his college entrance exams at Harvard. In France, Jack had a carbuncle surgically removed from under his left arm. Almost immediately, a serious bacterial infection set in, apparently caused by the

R. Cramer

The Lincoln sarcophagus. Robert Todd Lincoln was interred at Arlington in 1926. His wife and son, Abraham Lincoln II, are also buried at the site.

use of unsterile instruments during the surgery. Robert Lincoln had the boy returned to London to recuperate but Jack died on March 5, 1890, at the age of sixteen. His body was returned to Springfield, Illinois, where it was temporarily interred near his grandfather in the Lincoln mausoleum.

Robert Todd Lincoln became a successful businessman and a millionaire, living until 1926. Upon his death, he was buried at Arlington National Cemetery in a plot with a view of the newly constructed Lincoln Memorial. Mary Harlan, his wife of 58 years, was buried alongside him upon her death a decade later.

The remains of their son, Jack Lincoln, were reinterred to Arlington on May 27, 1930, but cemetery regulations would acknowledge a dependent's burial only in, "the records of the cemetery but the name shall not appear on any monument . . . [and may be indicated] only with a footstone, sunk flush with the ground." Thus, Jack's memorial was a small, partially obscured footstone bearing the initials "ALII" placed at the Lincoln gravesite. In December 1983, since cemetery regulations had been liberalized, Robert Todd Lincoln Beckwith, the only surviving grandson of Robert Lincoln, had the name of Abraham Lincoln II inscribed on the marble sarcophagus. Ironically, Beckwith died without an heir on December 24th, 1985, and the Lincoln line ended with his demise.

William Howard Taft

For a quarter of a century, from 1921 through 1948, there was only one state funeral conducted by the United States, that for former President and Chief Justice, William Howard Taft in 1930. Taft graduated from Yale University and gained a national reputation during his astute governorship of the occupied Philippine Islands after the Spanish-American War. He later served as Secretary of War under President Theodore Roosevelt and succeeded him as chief executive in 1909.

In the 1912 presidential contest, Taft was nominated for re-election by the Republican Party. The Democrats, in turn, nominated the popular governor of New Jersey, Woodrow Wilson. Former President, Theodore Roosevelt, frustrated in his efforts to become the Republican standard-bearer, mounted a powerful third party challenge, creating the Progressive or Bull Moose Party. Now, with the Republican vote hopelessly split between Taft and Roosevelt, Wilson handily won the presidency and Taft involuntarily retired, later stating, "I do not care for politics. Not that I have no interest in such matters, but because I am not fitted for the mustings and controversy."

Upon the return of the Republicans to office in 1921 under the Harding administration, Taft was appointed Chief Justice of the United States Supreme Court, thereby becoming the only man in history to hold the highest positions in both the executive and judicial branches. Taft excelled in the Supreme Court, delivering over 250 opinions but refusing to write any dissenting positions since he preferred not to disagree publicly with his distinguished colleagues.

In February 1930, at the age of 72, Taft retired from the bench because of a persistent heart problem exacerbated by his ample, 300-pound girth. A month later, on March 8th, the former President suffered a fatal stroke at his home in Washington, D.C.

On March 10th, a 48-gun salute to the Union was fired in his honor, the traditional acknowledgement of the death of a chief executive. Funeral plans were formalized by his family who, in accordance with Taft's wishes, selected a grave in a secluded location at Arlington National Cemetery.

President Hoover declared an official 30-day mourning period and Taft's body was brought to the Capitol to lie in state in the Rotunda. Funeral services were held on March 11th at the All Soul's Unitarian Church on 16th Street. The body was then escorted to Arlington for appropriate services.

R. Cramer

The grave of William Howard Taft, the 27th President of the United States. Taft was the first American chief executive buried at Arlington. The wreath in front of the monument was sent by President Ronald Reagan to commemorate Taft's 129th birthday.

Taft became the first American president to be interred at Arlington National Cemetery. Each year on Taft's birthday, September 15th, the incumbent president sends a wreath to the grave to be placed with full military honors. Similar services are held at all presidential gravesites on the deceased executive's respective birthday.

CHAPTER FIVE

Under My Eternal Vigilance

—Sentinel's Creed

World War I saw the development of new and terrible technologies from the machine gun to poison gases, all of which contributed to unprecedented human destruction. During the four years of sustained combat between 1914 and 1918, the warring powers suffered over eight million battlefield casualties. The civilian populations were forced to endure famines and epidemics while being subjected to constant shortages of food and medicine.

After the war, the British and French governments attempted to bring some meaning to the slaughter by interring an unknown soldier in a place of supreme honor to symbolically represent, and pay tribute to, all who had perished. In 1920, an unidentified English soldier was disinterred and returned from France in a simple pine coffin covered with the British Union Jack. The body was taken to Westminster Abbey for funeral services which were attended by King George V and thousands of widows and Gold Star mothers. During the extensive ceremonies, the King presented the British Unknown with a saber inscribed: "A British Warrior who fell in the Great War 1914/1918." The casket was finally committed to a specially prepared crypt in the abbey which had been filled earlier with soil taken from the battlefields of France where the British soldier had undoubtedly died.

Simultaneously, the French were entombing an Unknown Soldier from their nation at the base of the *Arc de Triomphe* in ceremonies planned to coincide with the British services. The *London Times* reported:

At the very hour when the Unknown British Warrior to 'the

noise of an Empire's lamination'—and proud rejoicing—was being borne to his last home at Westminster, an Unknown French Warrior, his faithful companion in arms was being carried to the *Arc de Triomphe* , there to remain throughout the ages as a symbol of that suffering and glory of which in his life and in his death he achieved his just share.

With the burials of the French and British Unknown Soldiers, other European nations which had participated in the Great War undertook plans to honor anonymous soldiers from their countries. The Italian ceremonies, conducted in Rome on November 4, 1921, were marred by factionalism and political dissent, a harbinger of future European hostilities. The *London Times* reported:

> Communists were in the crowds, wearing their badges with hammer and scythe; Fascisti, in black shirts embroidered with skull and cross-bones; mothers proudly displaying the medals won by their dead sons; little school children dressed in white, clustering around bespectacled priests; maimed soldiers who are carried on stretchers; blinded soldiers who wanted to hear though they cannot see the ceremony.

The United States did not undertake any substantive plans for the burial of an unknown soldier until after the conclusion of the 1920 presidential contest. Shortly thereafter, legislation sponsored by Congressman Hamilton Fish of New York was adopted, authorizing the return of an Unknown American Soldier from Europe and for burial at Arlington National Cemetery on the plaza of the newly completed Memorial Amphitheater.

American military involvement in World War I was brief, lasting only a single year. During that time, 99 percent of all American casualties were positively identified and buried in marked graves. Still, by 1921, there were 1,237 soldiers from the American Expeditionary Forces (AEF) whose remains were classified as unidentifiable. Four of these bodies were exhumed from different cemeteries in France, each denoting a theater of operations where American forces had been engaged. After it was verified that these anonymous soldiers had indeed fought with the AEF and that their deaths were combat related, they were officially declared candidates for the nation's Unknown Soldier.

The four bodies were placed in identical caskets and brought to Charlons-sur-Marne for the formal selection ceremony. Sergeant Edward F. Younger, Headquarters Co., 2d Battalion, 50th Infantry, U.S. Army, a highly decorated combat infantryman, was given the honor of choosing the American Unknown. Younger made his selection by placing a single white rose on one of the coffins. Later he commented: "I went into the room and walked past the caskets. I walked around them three times. Suddenly I stopped. It was as though something had pulled me. A voice seemed to say: 'This is a pal of yours.'"

The remains of the designated Unknown Soldier from World War I were taken to the port city of Le Harve for transport back to the United States. The cruiser *U.S.S. Olympia* , the famous flagship of Admiral Dewey, was commissioned to make the Atlantic crossing. The remaining unselected candidates were immediately taken to the Romagne Cemetery and reburied to ensure the perpetual anonymity of the American Unknown.

Interment services at Arlington National Cemetery were scheduled for Armistice Day, November 11, 1921. President Harding, honoring a Congressional Resolution, proclaimed the day a national holiday:

> Whereas Armistice Day, November 11, 1921, has been designated as the appropriate time for the ceremonies incident to the burial of the unknown and unidentified soldier in the Arlington National Cemetery . . .
> Whereas this unknown soldier represents the manhood of

National Archives

The caisson bearing the remains of the World War I Unknown Soldier at the Capitol. General John J. Pershing served as an honorary pallbearer.

America who gave their lives to defend its integrity, honor and tranquility against any enemy, and

Whereas the nations of the earth are on that date joining with the United States in paying respect and homage to this unknown soldier, therefore be it,

Resolved . . . [to declare] November 11, 1921, a holiday.

The *Olympia* arrived at the Washington, D.C. Navy Yard on November 9th and the casket of the Unknown was conveyed to the Rotunda to lie in state upon the Lincoln catafalque. A joint service honor guard was deployed around the coffin to maintain a continual vigil throughout the period of public viewing. During the next two days, while the Unknown Soldier laid in state at the Capitol, over 90,000 people quietly filed by the bier to pay their respects.

On the morning of November 11th, the casket was placed upon a horse-drawn caisson for the final journey to the cemetery. The accompanying funeral procession on foot was led by President Warren G. Harding and Chief Justice of the Supreme Court William Howard Taft. Former president Woodrow Wilson, still suffering the debilitating effects of a stroke, participated but was forced to ride in an open carriage.

National Archives

The committal services of the World War I Unknown at Arlington Cemetery. Chief Plenty Coup later removed his war bonnet and placed it on the Tomb in honor of America's "Unknown Warrior."

Huge crowds amassed along the funeral route watched solemnly as the coffin slowly passed. However, at the site of Wilson, spontaneous cheers disrupted the silence. The *New York Times* observed "It was apparent that the sight of Wilson, his once strong body broken by ill-health, his limbs too frail to permit his marching with the other great men who followed the Unknown caisson on foot, was a grim reminder that he had been an outstanding figure in the world conflict which today's ceremonial typified."

Upon reaching the White House, Wilson, physically unable to attend the burial rites at Arlington, was forced to leave the funeral procession. President Harding and members of the official party also decided at this point to drive the remaining distance to the cemetery.

The caisson and the remnants of the procession continued through Georgetown and crossed the Potomac into Virginia by way of the Aqueduct Bridge. Harding and the other dignitaries attempted to cross the river via the Highway Bridge located south of the city. An accident on the span, however, obstructed traffic and caused massive delays. Many of the dignitaries hopelessly abandoned their vehicles and decided to walk the substantial distance to Arlington, further contributing to the traffic problems. Others tried to commandeer small boats docked along the river in an effort to reach the west bank before the funeral services began. Even the presidential motorcade was stalled by the traffic jam. The *Washington Evening Star* reported, "the president's limousine had to mount the earth and circle through the grass plots of Potomac Park." Despite these heroic efforts, President Harding still arrived late at Arlington.

When the caisson reached the Memorial Amphitheater, the flag draped coffin was carried to the apse and placed upon a catafalque located on the stage. Over 5,000 people had crowded into the building for the funeral service while an additional 100,000 stood along the ridges of Arlington Heights, listening to the funeral ceremony over large loud speakers specially erected for the occasion by the Army.

After a two-minute period of silent tribute and a brief musical interlude, President Harding delivered the eulogy to the Unknown Soldier:

> Standing today on hallowed ground, conscious that all America has halted to share in the tribute of the heart and mind and soul to this fellow-American . . . it is fitting to say that his sacrifice, and that of the millions of dead, shall not be in vain. There must be, there shall be, the commanding voice of a conscious civilization against armed warfare.
>
> As we return this poor clay to its mother soil, garlanded by love and covered with the decorations that only nations can bestow, I can sense the prayers of our people, of all peoples,

The Tomb was placed under a daylight military guard in 1926. A decade later, the 24-hour vigil was established. The 50-ton marble cap stone was not added until 1932.

that this Armistice Day shall mark the beginning of a new and lasting era, of peace on earth, good-will among men.

At the conclusion of his remarks, President Harding awarded the American Unknown Soldier with the nation's two highest decorations for valor, the Congressional Medal of Honor and the Distinguished Service Cross. The casket was carried to the plaza area for the final committal services. Prayers were rendered by members of the clergy and the body was slowly lowered into the crypt layered with French soil.

Chief Plenty Coup, a Crow Indian representing all native Americans, stepped forward and spontaneously placed his war bonnet and coup sticks on the sarcophagus in tribute to the Unknown Soldier. The newspapers reported "When the aged Indian, with finely chiseled profile, removed his own feathered war bonnet and placed it tenderly on the marble edge of the sarcophagus and then lifted his arms in supplication toward Heaven, it constituted one of the outstanding features of the whole ceremony."

The Tomb of the Unknown Soldier soon became the most revered shrine to American servicemen. During its early years, the Tomb was protected only by a civilian watchman. In 1926, a formal military guard was established but was maintained only during the daylight hours when the cemetery was open to the public.

The original Tomb consisted only of the modest pedestal base. In 1926, architect Lorimer Rich was commissioned to design a more elaborate and suitable monument. A 50-ton piece of Colorado marble was positioned on the original structure and was then carefully sculpted to its present shape by Thomas Hudson Jones. The project was finally completed on December 31, 1931. On the front of the shrine are three figures representing Peace, Victory, and Valor. The phrase, "Here Rests in Honored Glory An American Soldier Known but to God" has been inscribed on the facade facing the Amphitheater. Although the author of these words remains unidentified, the same phrase is etched on the gravestones of all unknown soldiers buried in American cemeteries located throughout the world.

The Memorial Gateway

Throughout the cemetery's first 75 years of existence, access from Washington was limited to only two bridges across the Potomac River. A third span, constructed between 1926 and 1932, was designed to be a "memorial to American patriotism" and, according to the *Washington Evening Star* " . . . [united] the city of the dead with the political center of the nation."

The Lincoln Memorial commanded the eastern axis of the Memorial Bridge while the new Memorial Gateway to Arlington Cemetery provided its western terminus. The Memorial Gateway added two new entryways into the cemetery, the Schley and Roosevelt gates, named for Admiral Winfield Scott Schley, commander of naval forces during the battle of Santiago and President Theodore Roosevelt.

The Memorial Bridge and its mall approaches to Arlington National Cemetery symbolically united the North and South, forever dispelling the sectional differences that had earlier erupted into civil war. Arlington had become a place of national pilgrimage for the nation and an American national shrine. Judge Ivory Kimbell, a commander of the Grand Army of the Republic eloquently asserted, "Arlington is not for the burial of the soldiers and sailors of this generation alone. As long as the nation has armies and navies it will be used to bury its soldiers and sailor heroes."

World War II and Korea

After the outbreak of World War II, many individuals favored interring another unknown soldier at the Tomb to honor servicemen from that conflict. Initial planning for the burial was undertaken shortly after the Japanese surrender with interment tentatively scheduled for 1951. The World War II Unknown was to be buried in a duplicate tomb erected on the mall area just below the grave of his World War I compatriot.

In 1950, after the massive invasion of South Korea by Communist forces, all ceremonial planning ceased. Three years of combat followed and a cease fire was not arranged until 1953. Congress then authorized the entombing of two Unknown Servicemen at Arlington, representing the American veterans from World War II and from the Korean Conflict respectively.

By the end of World War II, 87,411 Americans remained missing. Many were lost at sea or killed in catastrophic air accidents. In Korea, 9,037 were listed as missing in action. These numbers included the 8,526 World War II and the 848 Korean War remains which were physically unidentifiable and buried without any knowledge of the victims' true identities. From these remains, the two new American Unknown Soldiers were selected.

For logistical reasons, the burials of the World War II and Korean Unknowns were to be conducted simultaneously on Memorial Day, May 30, 1958. It was also decided to bury the soldiers in two identical crypts flanking the grave of the World War I Unknown and to mark the burials with simple, flat, white memorial stones.

Greatly complicating the selection process of the World War II Unknown was the fact that the war had been fought in two diverse theaters. Since it was desirable that the representative Unknown should not be identifiable as to region, two World War II candidates—one from the Pacific Theater and one from the Europe/North Africa Theater—would be chosen. These bodies, in turn, would be brought together and made indistinguishable; one would be designated the Unknown Serviceman from World War II.

On May 12, 1958, at the Epinal American Military Cemetery and Memorial in France, 13 unidentified American remains from Europe and North Africa were brought together for the selection. Major General Edward O'Neill, U.S. Army, placed a wreath before one of the coffins, thereby designating the remains as a candidate for America's World War II Unknown Serviceman. Four days later at Hickam Air Force Base, Hawaii, six Pacific casualties were brought together. Colonel Glenn Eagleston, U.S. Air Force, similarly placed a lei on one of the coffins, thereby selecting the Pacific candidate. The Korean Unknown was selected by Master Sergeant Ned Lyle, U.S. Army, in separate ceremonies at the Punchbowl National Cemetery on the island of Oahu on May 15th.

The three bodies were transported to a predetermined location off Cape Henry, Virginia. There, all three bodies were brought on board the

U.S.S. Canberra where the remains were transferred to new, bronze caskets. The Korean Unknown Serviceman was brought to the deck of the ship and placed between the two World War II candidates who were then indistinguishable as to region. First Class William R. Charette, the Navy's only active duty Medal of Honor recipient, placed a floral wreath before one of the caskets, thereby completing the designation process.

During the ceremonies on the *Canberra*, Rear Admiral Levis S. Parks paid tribute to the three Unknown Servicemen: "These men did not fail us when the chips were down and we must not fail them in the days and years ahead when communist forces will press ever harder to drive the free world into slavery. It is not necessary that we know their names. It is enough that they were our comrades and shipmates." At the conclusion of his remarks, the remains of the unselected World War II candidate were buried at sea.

The Korean and World War II Unknown Servicemen were transferred to the *U.S.S. Blandy* for the final journey back to Washington, D.C. The ship docked at the Washington, D.C. Navy Yard on May 27, 1958. The Unknowns were guarded overnight by two sailors on the fantail of the ship. The following morning, the caskets were taken to the Capitol Rotunda to lie in state. Vice President Richard M. Nixon led the formal Congressional ceremonies.

On Memorial Day, May 30th, the caskets were placed on two caissons were taken to Arlington Cemetery. Along the funeral route, over 100,000 people watched the procession. As the caissons reached the Memorial Bridge, 20 jets flew overhead, minus one plane in the traditional missing man formation.

The funeral services held at the Memorial Amphitheater were attended by 216 surviving Medal of Honor recipients and were brief, hampered by the unseasonably hot temperature. Over 400 spectators collapsed during the ceremonies.

President Eisenhower did not deliver an address but did present the Medal of Honor to each of the Unknown Servicemen stating, "On behalf of a grateful people I now present Medals of Honor to these two Unknowns who gave their lives for the United States of America."

The bodies were carried to the plaza with President Eisenhower and Vice President Nixon positioning themselves before the respective coffins of the World War II and Korean Unknowns. The bodies were committed later that evening and memorial stones placed over the crypts after the cemetery had closed. They were later inscribed with the dates of American involvement in the two wars: 1941-1945 (World War II) and 1950-1953 (Korea).

The World War II and Korean Unknown Servicemen lying in state at the Capitol Rotunda, 1958.

Vietnam

As the nation was completing the burials of the two Unknowns, American involvement in the war in Southeast Asia was escalating. Motivated by the fear of communism's spreading throughout the region and jeopardizing American interest in the Far East, the United States began to send massive amounts of military aid to the non-communist government of South Vietnam. Likewise, as the war intensified, American military advisors were committed to the region to train the South Vietnamese military forces. By the end of the Kennedy administration in 1963, over 16,000 American troops were in Vietnam as non-combatants.

In 1965 after the Gulf of Tonkin incident, President Lyndon B. Johnson dispatched the first American combat troops to Vietnam. Ultimately, American troop strength peaked at 500,000 men. American forces were sustaining over 500 combat-related fatalities weekly. Domestically, the war became increasingly unpopular and opposition to American involvement swelled, primarily on the nation's college campuses. President Johnson, rather than risk political defeat at the polls, withdrew from the 1968 presidential contest, thereby conceding the presidency to the Republican candidate, Richard Nixon.

President Dwight D. Eisenhower and Vice President Richard M. Nixon at the double interment of the World War II and Korean Unknowns.

The Nixon administration pledged to bring about a swift and honorable end to the war and announced the policy of "Vietnamization." The policy called for the United States military to turn over responsibility for the war gradually to the Army of the Republic of South Vietnam [ARVN] while allowing the United States to disengage. By 1973, all American troops had been effectively withdrawn from South Vietnam. Two years later, the nation collapsed after a major North Vietnamese offensive resulted in the re-unification of the nation under a communist government.

As American involvement in Southeast Asia lessened, Congress authorized in 1973 the entombment of an American Unknown Serviceman from the Vietnam conflict. The Ford administration ordered the construction of a new crypt on the plaza of the Memorial Amphitheater between the graves of the World War II and Korean Unknowns. Plans for the burial, however, were suspended. Rapid helicopter evacuation and sophisticated identification techniques had resulted in the identification of all remains returned from Vietnam. Indeed, the pathologists at the United States Army Central Identification Laboratory in Hawaii proved to be remarkably skillful in identifying bodies through the use of dental records, superimposing photographs over skeletal remains, and blood typing.

It was not until a decade after the end of the war that one body was certified unidentifiable. On April 17, 1984, Secretary of Defense Caspar Weinberger announced that this soldier would be designated the Unknown Serviceman from the Vietnam Conflict and would be entombed at Arlington National Cemetery on Memorial Day.

For the first time since the custom of designating an Unknown Serviceman was established, no selection ceremony was possible. Instead, on May 17th, at Pearl Harbor, Hawaii, Sergeant Major Allan Kellogg, U.S. Marine Corps, a Medal of Honor recipient, placed a wreath before the single coffin officially recognizing the remains as the Unknown Serviceman from the Vietnam Conflict. The body was then placed on board a naval vessel and returned to the mainland.

The Vietnam Unknown Serviceman arrived in Washington, D.C., on May 25th. The remains were conveyed to the Capitol to lie in state over the Memorial Day weekend. During the three-day period, over 250,000 Americans visited the Capitol to pay their respects to the Unknown. On Memorial Day, May 28th, the coffin was placed on a caisson and transported to Arlington Cemetery, pausing briefly en route before the new Vietnam Memorial erected in tribute to the 50,000 Americans who had died during that war. As the procession crossed the Memorial Bridge, an unofficial delegation of Vietnam era veterans, dressed in military fatigues, joined the parade and followed the casket to the entrance of the cemetery.

At the Memorial Amphitheater, President Ronald Reagan delivered an eloquent eulogy to the Unknown Serviceman:

> The unknown soldier who has returned to us today and who we lay to rest is symbolic of all our missing sons . . . About him, we may well wonder as others have: As a child, did he play on some street in a great American city? Did he work beside his father on a farm in America's heartland? Did he marry? Did he have children? Did he look expectantly to return to a bride? We will never know the answers to those questions about his life. We do know, though, why he died. He saw the horrors of war but bravely faced them, certain his own cause and country's cause was a noble one, that he was fighting for human dignity, for free men everywhere. Today, we pause, to embrace him and all who served us so well in a war whose end offered no parades, no flags, and so little thanks . . . A grateful nation opens her heart today in gratitude for their sacrifice, for their courage and their noble service. Let us, if we must, debate the lessons learned at some other time. Today we simply say with pride: Thank you, dear son, and may God cradle you in His loving arms.

The body of the Vietnam Unknown Serviceman was buried in the center crypt, immediately in front of the tomb of the World War I Unknown. The white crypt cover was inscribed with the dates, 1958-1975, the period of American involvement in Vietnam.

Identification

In 1998, the family of United States Air Force Captain, Michael Blassie, requested that the military reopen its investigation concerning the identity of the Vietnam Unknown. Circumstantial evidence along with new advances in medical technology, indicated that the remains interred at Arlington could be those of any one of nine MIA's with the strongest evidence pointing towards either Capt. Blassie or U.S. Army helicopter pilot, Capt. Rodney Strobridge. Both men had been shot down on May 11, 1972, in a heavily jungled region near An Loc near where the Vietnam Unknown's remains were discovered by an ARVN patrol some six months later. The Pentagon, fully committed to a complete accounting of all servicemen still missing from the war in Southeast Asia, agreed to the disinterment in order to perform DNA testing on the recovered remains.

A plywood construction fence was erected around the crypt area at the Tomb of the Unknown Soldier while camouflage netting was positioned over the area to protect the dignity of the shrine. On the night of May 13/14, the marble crypt cover was carefully removed under the watchful eye of the Tomb Sentinels who maintained their vigil during the entire procedure. Before dawn the next morning, the casket had been removed and the plaza had been completely restored to its original appearance.

Evidence tape was placed around the Unknown's coffin and was then shrouded with a plastic rain cover. A new American flag was draped over the remains in preparation for the scheduled 1000 ceremony to be held on the plaza.

Secretary of Defense, William Cohen presided and acknowledged, "We disturb this hallowed ground with profound reluctance. And we take this step only because of our abiding commitment to account for every warrior who fought and died to preserve the freedoms that we cherish." Prayers were rendered and at the conclusion of the brief

U.S. Army Photo

A decade after the Vietnam Conflict had concluded, an Unknown from that war was interred at Arlington Cemetery. President Ronald Reagan delivered the eulogy during the funeral services in the Memorial Amphitheater.

U.S. Army Photo

After new advances in medical technology, the Vietnam Unknown was disinterred. A brief ceremony was held on the plaza with Secretary of Defense William Cohen delivering remarks. The remains were later identified as those of Captain Michael Blassie, USAF.

ceremonies, the flag-draped casket was carried by a joint service honor guard to an awaiting hearse, saluted by the Commanding General of the Military District of Washington and a Vietnam Medal of Honor recipient, Major General Robert Foley. From Arlington, the Unknown was transported to the Armed Forces Institute of Pathology at Walter Reed where MtDNA testing was to be performed. A few weeks later, the test results conclusively established that the remains were, in fact, those of Captain Blassie. They were then returned to his family for private burial at the Jefferson Barracks National Cemetery in St. Louis, Missouri.

After the identification of the remains, Secretary Cohen acknowledged, ". . . it would seem to me that given the state of art today, it's unlikely that we'll have future unknowns." The crypt of the Vietnam Unknown is now empty but the white memorial stone still remains on the plaza inscribed with the dates of the Vietnam Conflict, a silent testament to all of those who served during the war.

The Tomb Guard

The four Unknown Servicemen are under a 24-hour honor guard established in 1937. The 3d United States Infantry, "The Old Guard" assumed the duty of protecting the Tomb in 1948. Today, there are three reliefs of sentinels assigned to the Tomb. The soldiers are generally recruited from Fort Myer, Virginia, and must possess both an outstanding military record and an intense desire to become a member of the elite Tomb Guard. Likewise, all must meet the minimum six feet height requirement.

Prospective sentinels must first interview with the Sergeant of the Guard and the individual Relief Commander. If deemed acceptable, the soldier is assigned for a two-week probationary period where he is introduced to the numerous required duties. Once appointed to the Tomb, the "New Man" must continue his intense and rigorous training and is expected to work continually to perfect his uniform, to assist the other sentinels in preparing for their "walks," and to learn the history of Arlington Cemetery.

For the next several weeks, the "New Man" is trained by members of his relief in the "catacombs" located under the colonnade area of the Amphitheater. Initially, the soldier is permitted only night walks, a two hour shift after the cemetery is closed during which the Tomb is a restricted military area. Once deemed proficient, he is finally allowed to enter the relief's rotation and is permitted to guard the Tomb on a regularly scheduled basis throughout the day and night.

After nine months of duty, the "New Man" is given a battery of tests. His uniform and walk are carefully scrutinized by the other relief commanders and he is evaluated on his cemetery and military knowledge. If deemed proficient, the soldier is awarded the Tomb Guard Badge, a silver award which consists of an engraving of the Tomb, an inverted craven wreath, and the words "Honor Guard." The badge is prominently displayed on the right breast pocket of the soldier's uniform. After 12 months of honorable service at the Tomb, the "Badge Holder" is given permanent orders for the decoration and may then wear the Tomb Guard Badge for the duration of his military career, regardless of subsequent rank or branch of the service. Since its inception in 1958, less than 400 sentinels have successfully received permanent orders for the Tomb Guard Badge.

The soldiers at the Tomb are authorized three different uniforms— a blouse, an overcoat, and a raincoat. All are maintained by the individual soldier who must remove and polish all brass and insignia daily to the rigorous standards demanded by the relief commanders. The blouse is made of wool and is worn year-round despite the legendary heat of Washington summers; it is the only fabric that will adequately hold a crease in hot weather. The overcoat is worn only when temperatures are below 45 degrees and the raincoat during periods of inclement weather.

The uniforms, despite public perceptions, are not tailored; to give the uniform a smooth appearance, all excess material is carefully tucked into

The Changing of the Guard ceremony at the Tomb of the Unknown Soldier.

the mandatory 29-inch waist belt by assisting sentinels prior to the Guard Change. All the uniforms are dress Army blues reminiscent of the Continental regalia worn by the army during the American Revolution and the Union blue worn by federal troops during the Civil War.

Each soldier is issued a pair of sunglasses for use while guarding the Tomb. Although not a traditional part of the regulation military uniform, the sentinels are given a dispensation to wear the glasses since the bright, white marble can induce sunblindness and hinder their mission. The shoes worn by the sentinels are standard Army issue but additional layers of soles have been added to protect the soldiers' feet from heat and cold.

The black mat on the plaza in front of the crypt area, is 63 feet long and is replaced each Memorial Day. The sentinel on duty takes 21 steps across the mat, turns, and faces the Tomb for 21 seconds, representative of the highest military tribute, the 21-gun salute.

The Tomb Guard carries an M-14 rifle which is currently issued only to the members of the 3d Infantry and to selected sharpshooter regiments. The weapon weighs 9.5 pounds and is equipped with a chrome, ceremonial bayonet and a black mourning strap. The rifle is always maintained in a position between the visitors and the Tomb, indicating the soldiers' primary mission of protecting the shrine from intruders.

Each relief is on a three day duty rotation; that is, 24 hours on and 48 hours off. During the off hours, however, the soldiers are expected to practice continually, to prepare their uniforms, and to enhance their knowledge of the cemetery, all the while maintaining standard military skill and combat readiness. During the daylight hours, the Change of the Guard ceremony occurs on the hour in the winter months and on a 30-minute schedule during the summer. At night, the sentinel is on duty for a two-hour shift.

The origin of the ceremonial change is obscure; inspections tended to vary with the personalities of the individual sergeants. It is now a standardized procedure with only minor variations. The inspection is genuine. If a sentinel is deemed deficient, he will be ordered by the sergeant back to the quarters to make any necessary uniform corrections. The rifle is also checked for cleanliness by the sergeant who is careful to soak his white cotton gloves with water prior to the inspection to ensure an adequate grip.

Duty at the Tomb is voluntary and sentinels may leave to return to the company at any time. Most, however, chose to remain between 12 and 18 months and view their duty as the highlight of their military careers. Indeed, the sentinels believe their duty is a small tribute to the ultimate sacrifice offered by the four Unknown Servicemen to protect the ideals of the nation. Their belief is reflected in the Sentinel's Creed which is memorized by all of the guards and which encapsulates their feelings:

> My dedication to this sacred duty
> Is total and wholehearted
> In the responsibility bestowed on me
> Never will I falter
> And with dignity and perseverance
> My standard will remain perfection.
> Through the years of diligence and praise
> And the discomfort of the elements
> I will walk my tour in humble reverence
> To the best of my ability.
> It is he who commands the respect I protect
> His bravery that made us so proud.
> Surrounded by well meaning crowds by day
> Alone in the thoughtful peace of night
> This soldier will in honored Glory rest
> Under my eternal vigilance.

CHAPTER SIX

Your Sons and Daughters Have Served You Well

—Douglas MacArthur

The Tomb of the Unknown Soldier contributed to Arlington's stature as a national shrine, but as an operating cemetery, Arlington's appeal remained primarily regional. By January 1, 1941, 49,927 people had been interred on the grounds. The onset of World War II forever transformed Arlington because of the unique demands placed on the cemetery.

The United States belatedly entered World War II in December 1941 after the surprise Japanese attack on the American military and naval installations at Pearl Harbor, Hawaii. American soldiers were quickly deployed throughout the Atlantic and Pacific theaters in a massive two-front effort to thwart German and Japanese aggression. As American combat troops began to sustain heavy casualties, new military cemeteries were hastily established abroad to accommodate the growing numbers of war dead. Over 93,000 U.S. soldiers were permanently interred in 14 new national cemeteries on foreign soil. The vast majority of combat fatalities, however, were returned to the United States for burial in local cemeteries as specifically designated by family members. During this period, Arlington increasingly became the preferred burial location for thousands of war dead and interment levels swelled to an unprecedented annual rate of slightly over 2,000. The demand for grave space strained Arlington's limited land resources and the need for increased burial capacity once again became the major problem facing cemetery officials. In February 1944, the Associated Press reported that, "At the present burial rate the capacity of Arlington Cemetery will be exhausted in five to seven years . . . only 14,000 more persons can be buried in Arlington. There are about 55,000 graves there now."

In response to the crisis, the cemetery adopted a series of innovative polices designed to achieve maximum burial capacity. For the first time, the graves of minor children were located in a separate section, away from the plots of their parents since grave allotment for dependent burials required less space. Likewise, new grave plots throughout Arlington were universally reduced from the traditional, generous and aesthetic 6 feet by 12 feet to a more crowded but utilitarian 5 feet by 10 feet. Interments were permitted to within fifteen feet of roadways and the planting of new, large trees was radically curtailed to conserve valuable space. New interments were conducted throughout the cemetery in virtually all sections, including the older, more established areas without regard for any tract's historical era.

Foreign Nationals

Agreements concluded by the Allied powers required that host nations provide appropriate burial space for foreign military advisors and members of embassy delegations who died while on assignment in the United States during World War II. Eventually, 44 foreign nationals representing ten nations including Great Britain, the Netherlands, France, Greece, and Poland, were authorized burial at Arlington Cemetery. Most notable in this group was Sir John Dill, the head of the British military mission in the United States and a co-planner of the D-Day invasion. Because of his importance, his grave is marked with an equestrian monument, one of only two in the cemetery.

During the war, the United States initiated a limited policy of transporting captured German and Italian soldiers to various states to assist American farmers with harvesting crops. On the eastern shore of Maryland, several farms used this much needed labor resource. Three prisoners, however, died from illness during this period and, in accordance with provisions of the Geneva Convention, were provided with appropriate military funerals in a nearby government cemetery. Arlington, the closest national cemetery to Maryland's eastern shore, received the remains of the two Italians [Arcangelo Prudenza and Marlo Batista] and one German [Anton Hilberath] prisoner of war, all of whom were interred in Section 15C. Each year, on All Souls' Day, November 2nd, members of the Italian Embassy in Washington, D.C. continue to practice the Catholic custom of visiting the graves of the departed and come to Arlington to decorate the simple graves of the two Italian soldiers.

Ignace Paderewski

Ignace Paderewski, renowned composer, famed pianist, and Polish nationalist, fled to the United States in December 1940, an unwilling exile from his native country which had been overrun by the Nazis. Paderewski, serving as President of the deposed government, made repeated poignant appeals to the American people to supply aid to his besieged country.

On June 29, 1941, at the age of eighty, Paderewski died in New York. Allegedly, his last words were, "Poland will rise again." While Poland remained under German occupation, the composer's remains could not be returned for burial in his native Krakow. After being informed of Paderewski's demise, President Franklin Roosevelt, offered a temporary repose for the composer at Arlington Cemetery in the Mast of the *U.S.S. Maine* , for the composer "until Poland is free." The Polish Embassy gratefully accepted Roosevelt's proposal and Paderewski's remains were transported to Washington for a July 5th funeral service held in the Memorial Amphitheater. Afterwards, the casket was conveyed to the base of the Mast of the *Maine* where it was to be temporarily entombed. In 1944, the body of Manuel Quezon, the deposed president of the Philippines, was similarly allowed interment in the memorial until his body could be returned to the islands for burial after liberation from the Japanese.

Ironically, Paderewski suffered a different fate. The agreements reached at the Yalta conference in the winter of 1945 drastically altered

D. Reynold

Historian Philip Bigler recounts the history of Ignace Paderewski. The Polish composer remained at Arlington in temporary repose until the time when "Poland is free."

the post-war boundaries of Poland and allowed the Soviet Union to install a communist-backed government. The Truman administration declared that Poland was not yet "free," the criterion for the return of Paderewski's body to Krakow. For the remainder of the Cold War, the composer's body continued to rest in the Mast of the *Maine*, a hostage to international politics with no memorial to his presence.

Finally, twenty years after Paderewski's death, the music critic for the *Washington Post*, Paul Hume, wrote an article which reported, "It is an anomaly probably unique in history that the body of a man who was worthy to be called 'perhaps the greatest living man' lies today in a tomb that is wholly without any marking of any kind to indicate his presence there." The column spawned a renewed interest in Paderewski and on May 9, 1963, President John F. Kennedy attended ceremonies near the *Maine* to dedicate a memorial plaque to the composer. Kennedy reminded the gathered crowd of the reason for Paderewski's repose at Arlington, stating: "The understanding was that one day, when Poland would be free again, [Paderewski] would be returned to his native country. That day has not yet come. But I believe that in this land of the free, that Paderewski rests easily. We are proud to have him."

In 1969, the Archbishop of Krakow, Karol Wojtyla, visited Arlington National Cemetery and viewed the Polish composer's casket in the *Maine* memorial. A decade later, after Wojtyla's elevation to the papacy, he again returned to the United States as John-Paul II. The Pope's visit to America led to a large amount of diplomatic activity concerning a possible return of Paderewski to Poland should John-Paul wish to escort the great composer's remains back to Krakow. However, John-Paul was not able to include a visit to the cemetery and shortly thereafter, the liberal Polish labor union, Solidarity, was brutally suppressed by the communist government and an edict of martial law was imposed upon Poland. The political climate that had favored the return of Paderewski's body ended and would not be resurrected for over a decade.

As the 1980's came to a close, the world watched in amazement as Eastern Europe discarded forty years of Communist rule. In Poland, former shipyard worker and Solidarity leader, Lech Welesa, became the nation's prime minister. He quickly began to oust former Communists from his government and made a state visit to the United States in 1990. At that time, he visited Arlington and it was agreed that Paderewski's remains would be returned to Poland the following year, the 50th anniversary of his death. It wasn't until June, 1992, however, that the Polish government was ready for the transfer. On June 27, the composer's remains were removed from the *Maine* memorial and escorted to Fort Myer for a service at the Memorial Chapel.

A joint service funeral procession then escorted the casket to the Memorial Gate where it was transported to Andrews Air Force Base to be flown back to Poland.

Some fifty-three years after the Nazis had forced Paderewski into exile, he received an enthusiastic welcome from his countrymen. President George Bush spoke at a funeral mass in Krakow and eulogized, "Today is truly a homecoming: the day Poland welcomes home a part of its proud history, a great patriot and patron of freedom." Paderewski was finally laid to rest in a free and independent Poland.

Iwo Jima Flag-Raisers

On February 19, 1945, the United States Marines landed on the small, volcanic island of Iwo Jima, located just 650 miles southeast of Tokyo. The Japanese resistance was intense and continued for 36 days. The fighting eventually involved 75,000 American troops and cost a staggering 7,000 lives. An incredible 27 Medals of Honor were awarded for heroic actions on Iwo Jima, a measure of valor unprecedented in American military history.

U.S. Navy Photo

The Marine Corps Memorial located outside the northern entrance to Arlington Cemetery. Three of the Iwo Jima flag-raisers are buried at the cemetery.

During the early days of heavy fighting, members of the Fifth Marine Division were dispatched to scale the island's highest peak, Mount Suribaci. Once on the 550-foot summit, several Marines hoisted a small American flag. Because of the difficulty in seeing the colors, another group of six soldiers was dispatched to replace the first flag with a larger, more evident one. The soldiers—PFC Ira Hayes, PFC Franklin Sousley, PFC Michael Strank, Pharmacist's Mate John Bradley, PFC Rene Gagnon, and Corporal Harlon Block—were photographed raising the flag by Associated Press cameraman, Joe Rosenthal. Throughout the United States, the dramatic photograph of the American flag-raising on Suribaci appeared in newspapers and magazines and was subsequently adopted by the government as the official symbol for a forthcoming war bond drive.

The impact of the Rosenthal photograph led government officials to order removing the six soldiers who had participated in the flag raising from combat so that they could represent the military services as official spokesmen in the crucial fund-raising effort. Ironically, three of the soldiers had already been killed in action, including PFC Michael Strank whose remains were eventually returned to the United States for burial at Arlington National Cemetery.

Two of the survivors, Ira "the Chief" Hayes and Rene Gagnon, were paraded throughout the United States during the war's final bond campaign and became reluctant symbols of American military valor. The flag-raising photograph evolved into an American icon and was converted into a best-selling postage stamp. Subsequently in 1954, it was the model for the United States Marine Corps Memorial located just outside the northern entrance to Arlington National Cemetery.

Ira Hayes suffered many personal reversals and died in 1955. He became the second of the Marine flag-raisers to be interred at Arlington Cemetery. Rene Gagnon, the last surviving member of the Iwo Jima contingent, experienced similar misfortunes until his death in October, 1979. He was buried at Arlington, and at the behest of his family, his grave was located within a few hundred yards of the Marine Corps Memorial. A brass relief of the Suribaci flag-raising was mounted on the reverse of his government headstone with the inscription:

> For God and His Country
> He Raised our Flag in Battle
> And Showed a Measure of His
> Pride at a Place Called "IWO JIMA"
> Where Courage Never Died.

John J. Pershing

General of the Armies John J. "Black Jack" Pershing was confined to Walter Reed Army Hospital at the onset of World War II, unable to contribute to the nation's war effort. The valiant commander of the American Expeditionary Forces [AEF] during World War I was born just prior to the American Civil War in 1860. He attended the United States Military Academy at West Point and graduated in 1886. Pershing then served with the Army during the Indian campaigns against the Apache and Sioux tribes as well as in the Spanish-American conflict. He was sent to southwestern United States to apprehend the Mexican bandit, Francisco "Pancho" Villa, and with his forces, made several incursions across the border.

During this period, Pershing suffered a major personal tragedy when his wife and three daughters perished in a fire. Despite this loss, Pershing continued with his career and was placed in command of American forces destined for Europe. He steadfastly refused to allow dissolution of the AEF into separate commands under foreign generals and preached a doctrine of mobility. His strategy was successful in breaking the European stalemate by placing the Allied powers on the offensive and driving German troops from French soil.

U.S. Army Photo   R. Cramer

General Pershing wished to be buried among his men; a simple government headstone marks his grave. His grandson, Richard Pershing, was buried in an adjacent plot after he was killed in action in Vietnam.

At the conclusion of the war, to honor Pershing for his instrumental role in the victory, Congress promoted him to the rank of General of the Armies, a rank previously held only by George Washington. The act made Pershing the nation's highest ranking soldier, a position he held until his death in 1948 at the advanced age of 88.

The general had expressed a desire to be buried at Arlington National Cemetery and he had personally selected a plot near the graves of many of the soldiers he had commanded in World War I. After lying in state in the Capitol, Pershing's coffin was then placed upon a horse-drawn caisson and transported to Arlington Cemetery on July 19, 1948. The caisson stopped on the plaza of the Memorial Amphitheater before the Tomb of the Unknown Soldier in tribute to the anonymous World War I soldier who undoubtedly had served under Pershing's command. A brief memorial service conducted in the Amphitheater was attended by President Harry S Truman. The procession then proceeded to the gravesite where Pershing was buried. A standard, white government headstone, indistinguishable from the thousands of other American soldiers, was erected at his request. In 1968, in an adjoining grave, the general's grandson, 2d Lieutenant Richard Pershing, was buried after he was killed in action in Vietnam.

Arlington in the 1950s

On December 1, 1951, John "Jack" Metzler was appointed the new superintendent of Arlington National Cemetery. A stern but well-respected administrator, Metzler immediately took control of the cemetery and began to investigate ways to improve its operation.

Despite the increased popularity of Arlington and the continued large number of interments, all graves were still dug by hand. In 1955, Metzler announced plans to automate the process. He purchased two machines that were capable of, "open[ing] a grave in 12 minutes [while] a man with a shovel would take all day." In an interview with the *Washington Daily News* Metzler elaborated:

> 'The machine[s] also does a better job. The sides are smoother and the bottom of the grave is even. The machines dump the earth right into a truck, so the ground around the grave stays much cleaner . . . It costs around $29 to have a complete grave done by hand,' he said. 'With the Trenchmaster we've now got the cost down to $9 plus change.' No employes have been laid off because of the machines. They now have more time to maintain the cemetery's lawns and shrubs.

The physical appearance of the cemetery was greatly enhanced during Metzler's stewardship of Arlington. Indeed, the superintendent took daily two-hour inspection tours of the grounds, covering the entire ten miles of the cemetery's roads. With an incredible eye for detail, Metzler would later deploy the cemetery's landscaping crew to key areas that required attention.

The 21 years Metzler remained superintendent were among the most critical in Arlington's history. In 1959, the cemetery completed its 100,000th interment, once again focusing attention on the traditional space problems at Arlington. During the next decade, Metzler would be forced to implement a series of stringent eligibility requirements designed to restrict Arlington's burials. Likewise, he would be forced to prepare the cemetery for its most notable burial, that of John F. Kennedy, the nation's assassinated Chief Executive.

CHAPTER SEVEN

The Torch Has Been Passed

—John F. Kennedy

Arlington National Cemetery held special meaning for John F. Kennedy, the nation's thirty-fifth president, who saw the cemetery as a sacred place of burial for thousands of American veterans who had died for their nation's ideals. Dave Powers, formally the White House doorkeeper but, in fact, one of the President's closest confidants, remembered: "Jack was very quiet . . . whenever he would go to Arlington Cemetery. He would think of the sacrifices that so many people had made," including that of his eldest brother, Joe, who was killed in the explosion of his airplane during World War II.

On Armistice Day, November 11, 1961, President Kennedy made his first formal visit to Arlington to place a wreath at the Tomb of the Unknown Soldier. At the conclusion of the brief ceremony, the President delivered the keynote address before a gathered crowd of 5,000 people in the Memorial Amphitheater. The address began:

> We meet in quiet commemoration of a historic day of peace. In an age that threatens the survival of freedom, we join together to honor those who made our freedom possible . . . It is a tragic fact, that war still more destructive and still more sanguinary followed [World War I]; that man's capacity to devise new ways of killing his fellow men have far outstripped his capacity to live in peace with his fellow man.

Noting the nation's commemoration of the American Civil War Centennial, President Kennedy acknowledged the cemetery's historic origin:

President John F. Kennedy's last visit to Arlington Cemetery, November 11, 1963, just eleven days before his assassination.

This cemetery was first established ninety-seven years ago. In this hill were first buried men who died in an earlier war, a savage war here in our own country . . . These quiet grounds of this cemetery . . . remind us with pride of our obligations and opportunities. On this Veterans Day . . . let us pray . . . that there will be no veterans of any further wars, not because all shall have perished but because all shall have learned to live together in peace. And to the dead here, in this cemetery, we say they are the race, they are the race immortal.

Two years later, just eleven days before his assassination, President Kennedy again returned to Arlington for the 1963 Armistice Day services. Accompanied by his playful 3-year old son, John, Jr., the Presidential party was met by Major General Philip Wehle, Commander of the Military District of Washington, and was escorted to the Tomb for the traditional Presidential wreath-laying ceremony. Afterwards, Kennedy attended the scheduled memorial service in the Amphitheater but did not speak on this occasion. David Powers recalls that later, upon his return to the White House, the President was in a somber mood and at that time shared a personal letter he had recently received from a retired Marine Corps major. The major had recently written to the President thanking him for saving the lives of several members of his company 20 years earlier while in the Solomon Islands. Aboard PT-59, Lieutenant John Kennedy and his crew had made a daring rescue of a contingent of Marines who had been pinned down by heavy Japanese small arms fire on the island of Choiseul. One of the soldiers later died on board the PT boat in Kennedy's personal bunk and the major's letter had served to make the President's Arlington visit particularly meaningful as a tangible reminder of the human toll of war.

November 22, 1963

While on a campaign trip to Dallas, Texas, President Kennedy was shot and killed by an assassin on November 22, 1963. His death stunned the nation for no one was prepared for the demise of the young, vibrant, 46-year old Chief Executive. Indeed, the Military District of Washington (MDW), the agency entrusted with funeral arrangements for high government officials, had prepared no contingency plans for a Kennedy funeral. Matters were further complicated by the absence of the President's widow, Jacqueline, who had accompanied him to Dallas. Her immediate burial wishes for the President were unknown.

Kennedy's brother-in-law and the director of the Peace Corps, Sargent Shriver, arrived at the White House and began to prepare tentative arrangements for the President's funeral. Lieutenant Colonel Paul Miller, the chief ceremonies officer at MDW, was summoned to the executive mansion along with relevant documents from the last state funeral which had been conducted in 1958 for the Unknowns from Korea and World War II.

Among members of the administration, it was widely assumed that the President's burial would take place in Brookline, Massachusetts. Precedent strongly supported this assumption since at that time only two American presidents had ever been interred outside their native state. [William Howard Taft was buried at Arlington and Woodrow Wilson was interred at the National Cathedral, Washington, D.C.] Further supporting a New England burial had been the interment of President Kennedy's newborn son, Patrick, just 15-weeks earlier after the infant had died from congestive heart and lung failure. Kennedy had last visited the child's grave while on a trip to Boston on October 19th and, on that occasion, remarked to Dave Powers that the boy seemed so forlorn there, buried alone in the family plot. Thus, few intimates of the President could conceive of Kennedy's being buried elsewhere. Jacqueline Kennedy later remarked aboard Air Force One on the return from Dallas: "We'll bring them [Patrick and Jack] together, now," which was interpreted by many to mean a Boston burial.

At 4:55 EST on November 22, 1963, the Associated Press teletype prematurely announced, "President Kennedy's body will lie in state at the White House tomorrow . . . There's nothing definite yet on the funeral, but it's understood it will be in Boston." The *New York Times* went to press later that day with the story, "The President was expected to be buried at the Kennedy family plot in Holyhood Cemetery, near Brookline, Mass. He is a native of Boston."

Shriver, however, had to prepare for all possibilities since the President's remains were still en route to Washington. He contacted the Superintendent of Arlington National Cemetery, Jack Metzler, to inquire about potential burial plots. Metzler informed Shriver that ample grave space was available for the President's burial. He also assured the President's brother-in-law that Arlington would be ready should the Kennedy family decide upon a local interment. Immediately after the conversation, Metzler began to assemble the necessary staff who would be required to prepare for such an important funeral and ordered them to be available to work throughout the weekend.

The President's body finally arrived at Andrew's Air Force Base at 6 PM. A contingent of military pallbearers led by Lieutenant Samuel Bird had been dispatched to remove the casket from Air Force One, but members of the Secret Service and the Presidential party refused to allow the soldiers near the remains. Instead, several members of the Kennedy administration struggled with the heavy, bronze coffin until they finally loaded it awkwardly into an awaiting Navy ambulance for transport to Bethesda Naval Hospital.

Since military physicians were to perform the autopsy which was required because of impending criminal charges, Shriver likewise ordered Colonel Miller to assemble appropriate Armed Forces morticians to embalm and prepare the remains. Although military personnel were capable of the embalming procedure, the catastrophic nature of the President's wounds required the services of more skilled and experienced morticians and a private funeral home would have to be brought in to cosmetize the body. Miller recommended Gawler's Funeral Home, one of the oldest and most widely respected funeral establishments in Washington. Shortly thereafter, the firm's undertakers were dispatched to Bethesda to await their grim task.

Finally, the White House staff received the first formal statement from Mrs. Kennedy concerning burial plans. Her only expressed wish was to model her husband's funeral after ceremonies rendered for Abraham

Lincoln a century earlier. That evening, Professor James Robertson, the Executive Director of the United States Civil War Centennial Commission, was contacted by the White House and asked to complete the required research on the Lincoln burial. Robertson called David Mearns, the director of the Library of Congress, and arranged to meet him an hour later at the government repository.

The Library of Congress building had been routinely closed for the weekend and the office lights were inoperative since they were connected to a timer switch that prevented them from being used until the scheduled opening of the library the following Monday. Thus, armed only with flashlights, Robertson and Mearns descended into the stack areas rummaging through the library's extensive holdings for pertinent copies of *Frank Leslie's Illustrated* and *Harper's Weekly* which depicted the 1865 Lincoln funeral in graphic detail. Once he located the copies, Robertson took the material to the White House and carpenters used the century-old drawings to transform the East Room with mourning crepe.

At Bethesda, the autopsy and the preparations of the President's remains were not fully completed until 4 AM on November 23, 1963. A new, solid mahogany coffin had been purchased to replace the original, bronze Dallas casket which had been damaged during the hasty return of the Presidential party to Washington. Thirty minutes later, a Navy ambulance carrying the President's body slowly entered the White House grounds, saluted by members of a Marine honor guard detachment located along the North Portico entrance.

Lieutenant Bird and his six-member casket team moved forward and removed the President's coffin from the ambulance. According to military protocol, Bird was merely to supervise the transfer of the coffin, but the young Lieutenant quickly became aware that his team was having difficulty and was struggling under the enormous weight of the 1200-pound coffin. Ignoring military tradition, Lieutenant Bird stepped forward, grasped the end of the casket, and assisted his soldiers in conveying the remains into the East Room where the body was to lie in state while funeral arrangements were formalized.

November 23, 1963

Secretary of Defense Robert McNamara strongly contended that President Kennedy should be interred on federal property so that his grave would be readily accessible to the American people. At 6 AM on Saturday, November 23rd, he contacted Superintendent Metzler and requested to see potential burial locations at Arlington National Cemetery. Later that morning, McNamara was shown three plots—near the Mast of the *U.S.S. Maine*, at Dewey Circle, and on the slope below Arlington House.

Shortly thereafter, Attorney General Robert F. Kennedy arrived at the cemetery but he quickly eliminated the Dewey Circle plot as inaccessible and the *Maine,* location as inappropriate. The sloping hill below the Custis-Lee Mansion, however, seemed an ideal tract since the grave would be positioned along an axis line between the Lincoln Memorial and Arlington House—a site that would forever link President Kennedy with his martyred predecessor, Abraham Lincoln, and to American history through Robert E. Lee.

The final decision on the grave was left to Mrs. Kennedy who came to see the plot later that afternoon. After carefully scrutinizing the area for over 15 minutes, the President's widow nodded her assent and Metro Kowalchick, an Arlington employee, drove a tent stake into the ground to mark the approximate burial location.

Eugene H. Wilson, now General Foreman of Field Operations at Arlington, remembers that cemetery staff roped off the area to prevent tourists and reporters from approaching the site. Ground crews began the tedious task of removing mounds of leaves that had accumulated in the area. They also laid down cocomat runners and greens on the moist grass for the scheduled Monday services.

Once the cemetery was closed to public visitation, McNamara returned with Robert F. Kennedy to supervise the surveying of the grave. As work was progressing, the two men walked up the hill to Arlington House. There, a Park Service employee, Paul Fuqua, recounted that earlier that year, on March 3rd, President Kennedy and Charlie Bartlett had made an impromptu Sunday visit to the Custis-Lee mansion. After touring the house, Kennedy remarked that the view of Washington, D.C. was so magnificent that he could stay forever—a statement that seemed to indirectly confirm the Arlington site as an appropriate location for the President's grave.

November 24, 1963

At 12:30 PM, the President's flag-draped coffin was carried from the White House and placed upon a horse-drawn caisson for the procession to the Capitol Rotunda. Behind the caisson were the Presidential colors and Black Jack, the riderless horse which symbolized the demise of a fallen leader.

At the U.S. Capitol, Bird's casket team, now augmented by two additional soldiers, removed the coffin and carried it up the steep steps into the Rotunda where it was carefully placed upon the Lincoln catafalque. A short memorial service was conducted and eulogies were delivered by Speaker John McCormack, Senator Mike Mansfield, and Chief Justice Earl Warren. Warren called John Kennedy, "a great and good President, the friend of all men of good will, a believer in dignity and equality of all human beings, a fighter for justice, an apostle of peace." Kennedy's successor, President Lyndon B. Johnson, placed a floral wreath before the coffin which was now guarded by a continual detachment of four soldiers.

For the remainder of the day and night, thousands of private citizens were allowed to enter the Capitol to pay their final respects to the nation's thirty-fifth president, some waiting for over 10 hours in the cold and dark for a brief moment of silent tribute.

That Sunday at Arlington, cemetery officials were attempting to dig the President's grave but were hindered by the presence of gawking crowds and the news media. Metro Kowalchick remembered:

> We put up a plywood and canvas wall . . . We were trying to hide from the public, but the news media had rented helicopters and were flying overhead. We finished the sides [of the grave] with a long-handled shovel . . . We dug down seven feet, deep enough for Mrs. Kennedy to be buried there too. The soil was hard clay, there was a big oak tree. It's still there.

Mrs. Kennedy had expressed her desire earlier to mark the President's grave with an eternal flame similar to that of the French Unknown Soldier in Paris. Military personnel were unable to devise such an apparatus on short notice and instead contacted the Washington Gas Company. After extensive deliberations, the Gas Company fabricated a propane fed torch which could be safely lit by Mrs. Kennedy during the funeral the following day.

November 25, 1963

Lieutenant Bird was concerned about his casket team's performance. Although they had completed the Rotunda transfer with dignity, the body bearers would be expected on Monday to carry the extremely heavy coffin down the Capitol steps, again at St. Matthew's Cathedral for the Catholic funeral Mass, and finally at Arlington Cemetery for the graveside services. The slightest error would be forever documented and, at worst, could disrupt the solemnity of the funeral. Bird, therefore, decided that his team would have to practice to fully ready themselves for the impending task.

Privacy for Bird's team was imperative but reporters and newsmen were lurking throughout Washington, anxiously seeking an exclusive news story. Thus, it was decided to conduct the practice during the early morning hours at the Tomb of the Unknown Soldier which became a restricted military area once the cemetery had closed to the public. Furthermore, the site was ideal since there were numerous steps which would adequately simulate those of the Capitol and provide an ample challenge for the eight-member casket team.

Shortly after midnight on the morning of the 25th, Bird's soldiers arrived at the Tomb. A casket used at Fort Myer during honor guard training exercises had been commandeered and filled with sandbags. For the next hour, Bird's body bearers repeatedly carried the coffin up and down the steps at the Tomb, sometimes with the Lieutenant and another soldier sitting on top to add weight. The drill successfully restored the casket team's confidence and the next day they performed flawlessly.

Later that morning, virtually the entire nation watched the services for President Kennedy on television. At Arlington, however, cemetery employees conducted 23 other scheduled burials, each with appropriate dignity and military honors before the 3 PM state funeral of the President.

At the scheduled time, the long funeral procession entered the cemetery through the Memorial Gate. As the President's coffin was carried to the grave by Bird's casket team, members of the official funeral party gathered around the site, some intermingling with military personnel, greatly hindering the precise execution of honor guard commands. Still, the assembled crowd represented the greatest collection of dignitaries ever assembled at Arlington. Included among the mourners were President Charles de Gaulle of France, Chancellor Ludwig Erhard of the Federal Republic of Germany, Emperor Haile Selassie of Ethiopia, and Prince Philip of the United Kingdom. Overhead, 50 Navy and Air Force jets flew past the gravesite followed by the President's plane, Air Force One, which dipped its wing in final tribute.

At Mrs. Kennedy's request, a contingent of the Irish Guard stood opposite the grave and a Catholic committal service was performed by the Archbishop of Boston, Richard Cardinal Cushing. Cushing offered the prayer:

> Grant, O Lord, this mercy to Thy servant departed, that he who in his desires did Thy will may not receive the punishment of any misdeeds, and that as through faith that joined him to the company of the faithful here below, Thy mercy may make him the companion of the holy angels in heaven, through Christ our Lord, Amen.

The body bearers adroitly folded the interment flag and Superintendent Metzler presented it to Mrs. Kennedy. The young widow, assisted by Robert F. Kennedy, then used a torch to light the eternal flame, thereby entrusting the President to the American people. Upon the comple-

Jacqueline Kennedy, clutching her husband's casket flag, leaves the gravesite with her brother-in-law, Robert F. Kennedy.

tion of the formal services, several individuals lingered around the grave for a few moments, each silently saying good-bye to the President before departing the cemetery.

At 3:32 p.m., after members of the family had left, the casket was prepared to be lowered into the open grave. At that time, Superintendent Metzler was informed that members of the television news media were continuing to film and had ignored repeated requests to cease broadcasting. The lowering of a coffin is necessarily a logistical operation and is generally not seen by the public because the procedure would detract from the earlier, ceremonial parting achieved by the funeral service. Furious over the lack of cooperation from the media and intent upon maintaining privacy, Metzler ordered all electrical power shut off throughout the entire cemetery, thus effectively forcing the television networks off the air and allowing the casket to be privately lowered and the grave sealed.

The world's attention had been focused on Arlington during the President's funeral services and almost immediately the cemetery was deluged with letters of condolence and tributes to the President, many simply addressed to "the Site of the Eternal Flame." Innumerable rosaries, prayer cards, and poems were mailed to the Kennedy family, including hundreds of efforts, frequently inaccurate, to memorialize Arlington as the President's burial site. One representative tribute read:

> In eternal glory lie the mortal remains of our immortal President in Arlington National Cemetery.
> They rest on an open hillside among tall, bare elms, and a slight distance away stands a solitary cedar [sic].
> As one looks about from the grave of the President, one can see several hundred feet away thousands of our honored dead, and the floodlighted columns of the Curtis-Lee [sic] Mansion. One cannot help but sense a quiet, awesome feeling of deepest solemnity pervading the cemetery grounds.
> At the head of his grave burns an Eternal Flame, and around it is a multi-array of flowers.
> Let us trust that the light of this flame will cast its peaceful rays in the hearts of all men everywhere.

The Kennedy Gravesite

In accordance with Mrs. Kennedy's wishes, on December 4, 1963, the two deceased Kennedy children were reburied at Arlington—Patrick from Brookline, Massachusetts, and an unnamed daughter from Newport, Rhode Island. The *Washington Post* reported:

> Simple granite grave markers, taken from the original burial sites, have been erected for the two Kennedy children buried beside the late President Kennedy. To the right of the President's floral-banked grave is a small cross with the inscription 'Baby Girl Kennedy—August 23, 1956,' marking the spot of a stillborn child of the late President and Mrs. Kennedy. At the base of the cross are the words 'Suffer little children to come unto Me'. On the left side is a small marker with curved top for 'Patrick Bouvier Kennedy. Aug. 7, 1963—Aug. 9, 1963.' for the prematurely born baby, who died last summer.

The initial plot allotted for the President's grave was 20 feet by 30 feet and was completely surrounded by a white picket fence. Cemetery officials expected a large visitation at the grave but anticipated that tourism would slowly return to previous levels. During the first year, visitation at the Kennedy grave frequently reached 3,000 per hour and, on weekends, an estimated 50,000 people paid their respects daily. Incredibly, during the three years immediately following the President's death, 16 million

Aerial view of the Kennedy gravesite, circa 1964. Sixteen million people visited Arlington in the three years immediately following the President's death.

people came to Arlington in what Superintendent Metzler called, "the most tremendous demonstration [of respect in history]."

The large increase in tourism at the cemetery had negative aspects as well. In 1964, the *Minneapolis Tribune* reported,

> So many visitors have been coming to the late President's grave that picturesque old Arlington cemetery has been struggling to maintain its dignity. The reason is that, unfortunately, not all the visitors are well behaved. Vandals are stealing flowers off other graves, picnickers leave mounds of litter, tombstones are resting places for the weary, and irreverent kids play leapfrog among the rows of granite. While one couple stood chatting in the line, their daughter worked a crayon over the tombstone of Oliver Wendell Holmes.
>
> 'Some people simply fail to appreciate what Arlington stands for,' says cemetery Supt. John C. Metzler. To him, 'Arlington is the shrine dedicated to the military, and it contains the history of our country engraved in granite.'

R. Cramer

The Kennedy Memorial Grave was dedicated in March 1967. Around the ellipse are memorable quotations from the President's 1961 Inaugural Address.

The temporary walkways leading to the grave were grossly inadequate and plans to build a more suitable gravesite were begun early in 1964. The architectural firm of John Warnecke and Associates was commissioned by the Kennedy family to design and build the new memorial grave. Construction began in 1965 and continued for two years, often with Robert F. Kennedy stopping regularly at Arlington on his way to his Washington offices to supervise the process.

On the night of March 14, 1967, President Kennedy and his two deceased children were secretly reinterred to the permanent grave which was located directly below the original burial location. The new site was formally blessed the following morning by Archbishop Cushing and the short service was attended by Mrs. Kennedy, Senators Robert and Edward Kennedy, and President Lyndon Johnson. The *Washington Post* provided the following account:

> Without previous announcement, the caskets of the 35th President and his two dead children were raised from their temporary sites last night, carried about 20 feet downhill and reburied in the still uncompleted granite memorial. The 20-minute [dedication] service today was conducted in a driving rainstorm that pelted the participants as they huddled around

Cardinal Cushing, the archbishop of Boston . . . the service was conducted at 7 a.m., about an hour before the cemetery opened to the general public . . . At the conclusion of the private services, Mrs. John F. Kennedy placed lilies of the valley on her husband's grave.

The John F. Kennedy grave consists of Massachusetts granite quarried over 150 years ago and was personally selected by members of the immediate family. Sedum and fescue has been carefully planted between the stones to achieve the impression of a natural, New England granite field. Along the ellipse are inscribed several memorable quotations from President Kennedy's 1961 inaugural address. The entire area surrounding the grave was heavily landscaped with numerous flowering trees planted in the immediate vicinity to beautify the site.

The eternal flame remains the focal point of the memorial grave and successfully symbolizes the continued legacy of the President's ideals. His friend, Dave Powers comments:

No matter how many times I would drive by, I found my eyes attracted to that flame . . . and each time that I went by I said a prayer for the President . . . [The Eternal Flame] is a reminder to me of the greatest man I ever met and the best friend I ever had . . . the shame of the assassination is what might have been because today and tomorrow we shall miss him and we shall never know for sure how different this world might have been had fate enabled him to finish his agenda for peace.

Likewise, Melville Grosvenor, the editor of *National Geographic* eloquently wrote, "His life was such—the radiance he shed—that if we live to be a hundred, we will remember how he graced this earth and how he left it . . . but the deeds, the words, the examples of the man remain—and there will always be a flame to remind us."

Robert F. Kennedy

Robert F. Kennedy, the 42-year old Senator from New York, announced his candidacy for the presidency on March 17, 1968. His decision to seek the nation's highest elective office was prompted primarily by events in Vietnam, a conflict that Senator Kennedy saw as a squandering of American resources while diverting the nation's attention from pressing domestic problems including poverty and unemployment.

During the following weeks, Robert Kennedy's campaign for the Democratic nomination gained momentum, greatly aided by President Lyndon Johnson's surprise decision not to seek re-election. On June 5th,

Senator Kennedy won a climactic victory in the California primary. Shortly after delivering a triumphal speech to a group of campaign workers at the Ambassador Hotel in Los Angeles, he was shot and seriously wounded by a young Jordanian, Sirhan Sirhan, who opposed the Senator's outspoken support for the state of Israel.

Bobby Kennedy clung to life for the next 24 hours, but despite heroic life-saving efforts, the head wound he sustained proved fatal and the Senator died on June 6th. His body was flown to New York City where it laid in state at St. Patrick's Cathedral on 5th Avenue.

When informed of Kennedy's demise, Arlington Cemetery officials did not initially expect the Senator to be buried at the cemetery since a series of more rigorous eligibility requirements had been implemented the previous year. However, further investigation proved that Kennedy was, in fact, qualified for interment at Arlington as a former cabinet official with prior military service. Family members soon requested Robert Kennedy's burial be near the John Kennedy grave since the two brothers had been virtually inseparable during their lives. However, the Senator's widow, Ethel, requested that military participation in the services be held to a bare minimum.

The funeral Mass for Senator Kennedy was conducted at St. Patrick's Cathedral on Saturday, June 8th. It was attended by over 2,000 people, including all the major presidential contenders—Eugene McCarthy, Hubert Humphrey, and Richard Nixon. In the most memorable and moving address of his career, Senator Edward Kennedy eulogized:

> My brother need not be idealized, or enlarged in death beyond what he was in life, to be remembered simply as a good and decent man, who saw wrong and tried to right it, saw suffering and tried to heal it, saw war and tried to stop it.
>
> Those of us who loved him and who take him to his rest today pray that what he was to us and what he wished for others will some day come to pass for all the world.
>
> As he said many times, in many parts of this nation, to those he touched and who sought to touch him: 'Some men see things as they are and say why. I dream things that never were and say why not.'

At the conclusion of the service, the casket was placed aboard a special train for transport back to Washington, D.C. for the committal services at Arlington. The twenty-one car funeral train was scheduled to pass through the major East Coast cities of Newark, Camden, Philadelphia, and Baltimore, analogous to the journey of the Lincoln funeral train of a century earlier. The Senator's coffin was carefully positioned on a platform in the last car so that it could be seen by the thousands of expected mourners with a member of the Kennedy family maintaining a constant vigil.

No one anticipated the huge outpouring of grief that became apparent as the train slowly passed through New York. Thousands of people quietly gathered along the tracks to glimpse the Senator's coffin, many weeping while others passively held small American flags. Tragically, in Elizabeth, New Jersey, a large group of people failed to see an approaching northbound train and, in the ensuing panic, two people were struck by the oncoming train and instantly killed. Informed of the horrible accident, the Kennedy family ordered their train further slowed and all northbound traffic between Washington and New York was stopped.

Aboard the funeral train were over 700 people, including Senator Kennedy's widow and ten children. The atmosphere was that of an Irish wake where, in Theodore White's words, "[the mourners attempt to] make a man come alive again in the affection and memory of his friends."

The train, hopelessly behind schedule, did not arrive at Washington's Union Station until 9:10 PM, having required 8-1/2 hours to make the 225-mile journey from New York. Darkness was already descending upon the capital and Arlington had begun preparations for an unprecedented nighttime funeral. Floodlights had been strategically deployed around the open grave and military personnel had obtained 1,500 candles from nearby St. Matthew's Cathedral for the expected mourners.

The funeral procession formed at the train station and Senator Kennedy's casket was removed by thirteen civilian pallbearers, including former astronaut John Glenn, former Secretary of Defense Robert McNamara, family friend Maxwell Taylor, Robert's eldest son Joe Kennedy, and the sole surviving brother Senator Edward Kennedy. The funeral route was designed to pass the major government buildings of Robert's political career including the Capitol and the Department of Justice. When the motorcade reached the Lincoln Memorial, the hearse stopped briefly while the Marine Corps band played "The Battle Hymn of the Republic."

Finally arriving at the gravesite at 10:30 PM, the casket was borne to the grave by the thirteen pallbearers and a brief 15 minute service, illuminated only by floodlights and the flickering candles of the mourners, was conducted by Archbishop Terrence Cook. At the conclusion of the ceremony, the interment flag was carefully folded by John Glenn and presented to the Senator's widow by her son, Joe.

The grave of Robert F. Kennedy marked by a simple, white Christian cross was located only about 20 feet from the grave of his brother. A more suitable and elaborate memorial was desired by family members and the architect I.M. Pei, who would later design the East Wing of the National

Gallery of Art and the John F. Kennedy Library, was commissioned to devise drawings for the new grave.

In 1971, construction was completed on the memorial and Robert Kennedy's remains were reinterred to the present site, still adjacent to the grave of the John Kennedy. A Christian cross still marks the grave and along the fountain area are inscriptions from two of Robert Kennedy's most notable addresses. Each year, the graves of both Robert and John Kennedy are visited by over 3 million people.

Jacqueline Kennedy Onassis

In January, 1994, Jacqueline Kennedy Onassis learned from her doctors that she had contracted non-Hodgkin's lymphoma. Despite aggressive treatment, the former First Lady died from her illness a few months later on May 20 at the age of 65. The following day, Arlington National Cemetery officials were notified of the family's desire for an interment at the Kennedy gravesite. Plans were immediately begun for a private committal service, and the gravesite was closed to public visitation over the weekend to prepare the crypt.

On Monday, May 23, a funeral Mass was conducted in New York City after which the casket was flown to Washington, D.C. where a motorcade awaited. The solemn procession arrived at Arlington at 1:40 in the afternoon on a blistering hot May day. President Clinton greeted the surviving Kennedy children—Caroline Kennedy Schlossberg and John F. Kennedy, Jr.—as their mother's casket was carried to the gravesite by eight civilian pallbearers. There, a short, private service was conducted while a television crew located a discreet distance away, provided pool coverage to the nation.

When the gravesite re-opened the following morning, thousands of people quietly made their way to the site, some patiently waiting for over two hours to pay their final respects. A few weeks later, a bronze memorial plaque was added to the grave. It read:

Jacqueline Bouvier Kennedy
Onassis
1929–1994

CHAPTER EIGHT

May God Cradle You in His Loving Arms

—Ronald Reagan

Despite the massive efforts to conserve grave space during the previous two decades, it was apparent that Arlington would still be forced to cease burial operations by the late 1960s unless even more drastic policies were implemented. Thus, in 1961, Arlington became the first national cemetery to abolish the traditional practice of side-by-side interments for family members and adopted an experimental tier burial policy. An eligible veteran, spouse, and all dependents were allotted a single grave with burials accomplished through stacking or offsetting the various coffins. The tier system instantly doubled Arlington's existing burial capacity and soon proved so efficient that the practice was mandated for the entire national cemetery system the following year.

In 1967, to supplement the tier system, other grave conservation efforts were also adopted at Arlington. The Army imposed a series of stringent eligibility requirements which severely restricted in-ground burial to only a select number of servicemen. The controversial new criteria allowed interment for only those who died while on active duty; individuals who qualified for retirement benefits; Medal of Honor recipients; holders of the Distinguished Service Cross, the Silver Star, the Purple Heart, or comparable decorations; and spouses and dependents of the same.

The immediate need for additional space was alleviated somewhat when the cemetery made its most important land acquisition in 1966. The Fort Myer South Post was formally ceded to Arlington to expand the cemetery's grave facilities. The military installation, which adjoined Arlington's eastern boundary, encompassed 190 acres of land. Its dilapidated World War II-era buildings were quickly razed while extensive land-scaping was undertaken to beautify the area to prepare it for future buri-als. With the addition of the South Post acreage, Arlington's size swelled to 612 acres, ensuring the continued operation of the cemetery until ap-proximately 2020.

Vietnam

For most Americans, the image of the Vietnam Conflict was restricted to graphic scenes of combat televised daily during the evening news. Arlington, however, was experiencing the tangible human residue of that conflict. Indeed, during the late 1960s when American forces were sustaining well over 500 combat-related fatalities weekly, interments at Arlington correspondingly increased. Thurman Higginbotham, who worked as a cemetery representative during the war, remembers that the six member interment staff was routinely handling between 30 and 37 burials daily. On one occasion, the cemetery performed an unprecedent-ed 47 funerals, a level never again duplicated.

The Vietnam Conflict never gained the complete support of the Ameri-can public and, as casualties began to mount, funeral services for those killed in the war were commonly marred by bitterness. Indeed, young widows, parents, and relatives of the deceased, overcome with grief, frequently refused to accept the triangular folded casket flags. Some be-reaved families severely restricted military participation in the services.

Relatives of many servicemen who were missing in action or whose remains were never recovered from Vietnam were allowed to erect small government memorial stones to their loved ones. Each marker begins with the identical inscription, "In Memory of . . ." Over 2,000 service-men remained unaccountable after the Vietnam Conflict and entire new sections reserved for the bodiless graves had to be created marked only by such cenotaphs.

While Arlington was attempting to conduct an unprecedented num-ber of funerals, visitation levels had simultaneously peaked after the in-terment of President John F. Kennedy. The cemetery remained open to civilian traffic and on some days, over 5,000 cars and buses would rou-tinely drive through the cemetery, clogging roads and frequently inter-fering with ongoing funeral processions. A study commissioned by the Department of the Army reported, "Auto congestion, noisy buses within the gates, and tourists in holiday mood contradict the atmosphere of dignity and repose." In 1970, in an effort to respect the grief of families in mourning, the cemetery was permanently closed to private vehicular traffic.

The *U.S.S. Forrestal*

The United States began its heaviest bombing raids of the war against major military targets in North Vietnam in 1967. The carrier, *U.S.S. For-*

U.S. Navy Photo

In 1967, a missile exploded on the U.S.S. Forrestal. *Eighteen members of the crew were buried in a group grave at Arlington.*

restal, was dispatched for the first time to the Tonkin Gulf to provide additional planes for the airstrikes. On July 29, while the *Forrestal* was in the process of launching several heavily armed aircraft, one of the plane's jet exhausts ignited a missile on a nearby fighter, exploding a fully loaded auxiliary fuel tank. The fire quickly spread throughout the flight deck and below deck compartments, detonating tons of ammunition.

The 4,300 men of the *Forrestal* crew heroically battled the intense flames for over 14 hours while escort destroyers moved precariously to within 10 feet of the burning carrier to spray thousands of gallons of water on the flames. The heavily damaged *Forrestal* limped slowly back toward port in the Philippines while the crew began the gruesome task of accounting for missing sailors. The *Washington Post* reported:

> Some [Navy personnel] were burned to ashes fighting the blaze or trying to escape from their burning planes. Some were blown into the sea by bomb explosions and others are sealed in compartments below the flight deck where they were sleeping when the fire began . . . Crewmen continued to search the 76,000-ton carrier for bodies, hacking through

bulkheads and wading through water-filled passageways still
warm from the flames of the burning fuel that poured down
openings into the lower decks of the ship.

Twenty-one jet aircraft had been destroyed in the fire and an additional 42 were heavily damaged. In the worst Naval disaster since World War
II, 129 men were killed. Eventually, 18 of the deceased were buried at
Arlington Cemetery in Section 46. Since their remains were burned beyond recognition, they were interred together in a common grave with a
single headstone bearing the inscription "Died in Fires and Explosions—
U.S.S. Forrestal, July 29, 1967."

The U.S.S. Liberty

In June 1967, an unarmed intelligence ship, the *U.S.S. Liberty*, was
dispatched to the Middle East to monitor the ongoing communications
between belligerents during the Arab-Israeli War. While in international
waters and conspicuously displaying the American flag, the *Liberty* was
repeatedly attacked by heavily armed Israeli jet fighters with missiles and
napalm.

Virtually defenseless, the American vessel desperately radioed for assistance from the U.S. Sixth Fleet. The carrier *America* dispatched four

U.S. Navy Photo

*The intelligence ship U.S.S. Liberty listing badly after a combined missile and torpedo assault by
Israeli forces during the 1967 Arab-Israeli War.*

combat-ready F-4 fighters to the scene. When Secretary of Defense Mc-Namara was informed that the American planes were equipped with nuclear weapons, the aircraft were immediately recalled, leaving the *Liberty* to weather the assault alone.

The attack on the *Liberty* was soon joined by two Israeli patrol boats while the crew, unaware of developments, anxiously awaited air support. A torpedo hit the vessel's starboard side and ripped a 40-foot hole in the ship's hull, instantly killing 25 members of the crew.

Several hours after the incident, the Israeli government sent apologies to the United States, claiming that the *Liberty* had been mistakenly identified as a potentially hostile vessel. In a subsequent formal notification delivered to the American government, Israel stated, "its since expression of deep regret for the tragic accident in which, at the height of hostilities in the area, the *U.S.S. Liberty* was hit by Israeli fire."

Israel eventually paid $3.5 million in reparation to the families of the 34 American sailors who were killed and a similar sum to the 171 wounded servicemen. Inexplicably, the United States seemed content to dismiss the attack and accept the Israeli version of the incident while virtually ignoring the testimony of the *Liberty* officers and men which proved conclusively that the attack on the ship was both deliberate and premeditated. In his memoirs written four years after the event, President Lyndon Johnson inaccurately summarized the entire episode: "Ten men of the *Liberty* crew were killed and a hundred were wounded [sic]. This heartbreaking episode grieved the Israelis deeply, as it did us . . . Aside from the tragic accident involving the *Liberty*, no American died in the Middle East war in 1967."

The remains of 14 members of the *Liberty* crew, including the ship's Executive Officer, LCDR Philip Armstrong, were taken to Arlington National Cemetery for burial. Three of the bodies were individually unidentifiable and were thus buried under a group headstone listing the names of the six missing servicemen of the *Liberty* crew. Philip Ennes in his book, *The Assault on the Liberty*, recounts, "Three men, apparently swept away and into the sea, could not be accounted for. Three others could not be identified. These were eventually buried, along with stray limbs and other unidentifiable parts, in a mass grave at Arlington National Cemetery."

The group marker was originally engraved with the terse inscription "Died in the Eastern Mediterranean." After years of petitioning, the United States Navy agreed to provide a more appropriate epitaph. The new headstone was finally erected in October 1982, 15 years after the original incident.

In his address during the unveiling ceremonies Commander X. Bender Tansill explained:

The new headstone carries this epitaph—'Killed—*U.S.S Liberty*-June 8, 1967.' We now know that these six crew men were killed. Perhaps it would have been better to have included the words 'in combat' but now we know from the epitaph that they were killed on the *U.S.S. Liberty*, they did not just die in an Eastern Sea . . . These five sailors and one Marine did not just die! They were deliberately killed on board of the *U.S.S. Liberty* when that ship of our Navy was intentionally attacked without warning . . . These six crewmen were blown to pieces when the torpedo struck the *U.S.S. Liberty* and blew a hole in it, 40 feet long below the waterline.

Audie Murphy

The July 16th, 1945 cover of *Life* Magazine featured "The Most Decorated Soldier" of World War II, Audie Murphy. Murphy, as a boy from Farmville, Texas, had lied about his age in 1942 to enlist in the United States Army as a private. During the military campaigns in Sicily, Italy and Germany, he was rapidly promoted to the rank of Second Lieutenant for his valorous battlefield conduct and was awarded 24 decorations including the nation's highest, the Congressional Medal of Honor. The accompanying citation detailed Murphy's bravery while in Germany:

> With [6] enemy tanks abreast of his position, 2d Lieutenant Murphy climbed on [a] burning tank destroyer, which was in danger of blowing up at any moment, and employed its .50 caliber machine gun . . . his deadly fire killed dozens of Germans . . . [Murphy] received a leg wound, but ignored it and continued the single-handed fight until ammunition was exhausted . . . 2d Lieutenant Murphy's indomitable courage and his refusal to give an inch of ground saved his company from possible encirclement and destruction, and enabled it to hold the woods which had been the enemy's objective.

After the war and his release from the Army, Murphy published an autobiographical account of his war experiences entitled, *To Hell and Back* which was adapted by Hollywood into a feature length drama in which Murphy portrayed himself. Murphy went on to star in 40 motion pictures during his acting career but a failed marriage and financial difficulties tarnished his reputation. His life ended tragically in 1971 when the small private plane in which he was traveling crashed in the Blue Ridge Mountains of Virginia.

The United States Army accorded its most decorated soldier a funeral with full military honors at Arlington National Cemetery. The graveside services were attended by United Nations Ambassador, George Bush, officially representing President Richard Nixon who honored Audie Murphy in an official proclamation:

> [Audie Murphy] came to epitomize the gallantry in action of America's fighting men . . . When challenged to defend their freedom, Americans have always stood ready to defend it with courage and daring, and each war in which the nation has been engaged has produced its own special heroes . . . As America's most decorated hero of World War II, Audie Murphy not only won the admiration of millions for his own brave exploits, he also came to epitomize the gallantry in action of American fighting men. The nation stands in his debt and mourns at his death.

Audie Murphy's grave is situated in the immediate vicinity of the Memorial Amphitheater. Shortly after his burial, several proposals were submitted for a more elaborate memorial at the Arlington gravesite, many bordering on ostentation. Murphy's widow, however, tastefully refused all such plans and consented only to a modest walkway leading to her husband's simple grave, marked at her behest with a white government headstone.

The Bicentennial

Mr. Raymond J. Costanzo, a World War II veteran who had served with the 508th Parachute Infantry, 82nd Airborne Division, during the Normandy invasion, was appointed the new superintendent of Arlington Cemetery on May 18, 1975. His first major task was to ready the cemetery for the forthcoming Bicentennial celebrations commemorating the 200th anniversary of the founding of the United States.

A much needed renovation of the Memorial Amphitheater was undertaken to accommodate the numerous tourists and foreign visitors expected to come to Arlington during the Bicentennial year. Repairs to the structure and the addition of facilities for the handicapped were completed. To enhance the physical appearance of the cemetery, Mr. Costanzo also established a rigorous and ongoing policy of straightening and realigning of headstones while the overall maintenance and landscaping of the grounds were greatly improved.

During 1976, virtually every major head of state from the free world, including Queen Elizabeth of Great Britain, King Juan Carlos of Spain, and Emperor Hirohito of Japan, visited the United States and paid honor to American veterans by placing a wreath at the Tomb of the Unknown Soldier.

The Veterans' Administration approved new, government headstones inscribed with gold leaf lettering to specifically honor deceased Medal of

Honor recipients during the nation's celebrations. Throughout Arlington, all of the headstones of Medal of Honor recipients were replaced with the new, Bicentennial markers. Only Audie Murphy's grave was excepted at the behest of his widow who declined a replacement stone.

Also during the Bicentennial, Mr. Costanzo created a Historian's Office to document the various services and ceremonies conducted at the cemetery. The superintendent remembers that "bits and pieces of historical documents . . . [had] been gathering dust, rolled up in somebodies drawer . . . [and]getting it put into some type of order [was a major priority.]" Thus, the office began a preservation program to safeguard many of Arlington's priceless artifacts.

When the historians began the massive task of gathering and organizing the cemetery's extensive historical documents and records, they discovered that Arlington's original burial records, dating from 1864, had been unwisely stored in an unused crypt at the Memorial Amphitheater. All of the volumes were suffering from damaging effects of moisture and mold which, if unchecked, could destroy the irreplaceable volumes. Mr. Costanzo, after being informed of the situation, authorized the construction of a new storage facility with controlled temperature and humidity to house the collections. A rare book expert from the Library of Congress was consulted to assess the damage to the material. He was eventually commissioned to begin the delicate restoration and preservation of the volumes.

Hostage Rescue Mission

In 1979, the deposed Shah of Iran entered the United States to seek treatment for cancer. His visit spurred Islamic fundamentalists to storm the American Embassy in Teheran and seize 53 American citizens as hostages, demanding the Shah's return to his native country. The Carter administration attempted to negotiate the release of the Americans. After months of frustrating and futile deliberations with the Ayatullah Khomeini's revolutionary government, the President approved a dramatic plan to rescue the American captives.

One hundred eighty American servicemen secretly practiced for four months the intricate maneuvers that would be required to land an American commando force deep in Iranian territory and eventually liberate the hostages. When the plan was implemented on April 25, 1980, however, a series of unfortunate accidents doomed the mission to failure.

Eight helicopters and six C-130 transport planes were first scheduled to rendezvous at a predetermined desert location 250 miles east of the Iranian capital. Two of the helicopters were unable to reach their destination because they were disabled by a sudden desert sandstorm. A third craft developed hydraulic problems shortly after landing in the staging area and was unable to proceed to Teheran. With the rescue operations requiring a minimum of six fully operational helicopters, mission commanders wisely decided to abort the rescue mission. While attempting to refuel for a return to their respective bases, one of the helicopters crashed into a transport plane, exploding and killing eight men. Fearing detection, the remainder of the force was quickly loaded on board the remaining planes and flown out of Iran.

The following day, the Iranian government photographed the disaster area. The charred remains of the eight American servicemen were taken to Teheran and placed on public display, desecrated, and commingled by angry mobs.

President Carter sadly announced the failure of the mission and fully accepted blame for the incident, "It was my decision to attempt the res-

P. Bigler

Three members of the Iranian Hostage Rescue team were buried at Arlington in 1980 after a series of catastrophes ended the mission. In 1986, the Iranian government issued a malicious postage stamp commemorating the "Failure of U.S. Military Aggression."

cue operation. It was my decision to cancel it when problems developed. The responsibility is fully my own."

On May 9th, President Carter attended memorial services at Arlington National Cemetery for the eight servicemen who had been killed in the mission. In an address to the mourners, Carter quoted Robert E. Lee extensively stating, "Duty is the sublimest word in our language. Do your duty in all things. You cannot do more, you should never do less." He went on to praise the courage of the American servicemen. One of the mourners later recalled that Major Richard Bakke, U.S.A.F., one of the pilots killed during the mission, "looked forward with enthusiasm and anticipation to this last opportunity to serve not for the glory it offered but for the deep satisfaction of defending that which is good and decent."

Several weeks later, the bodies of the eight Americans were returned to the United States. The remains of Major Bakke, Major Harold Lewis, U.S.A.F., and TSG Joel Mayo, U.S.A.F., were individually unidentifiable and were consigned to a single coffin and buried at Arlington National Cemetery in Section 46 near the Memorial Amphitheater. A white marble monument with a bronze memorial plaque was erected nearby in 1983 in tribute to all of the men who died in the noble effort to rescue the American hostages.

Joe Louis

Joe Louis won the coveted heavyweight boxing title in 1937 and held the championship longer than any other individual, forfeiting it only upon retirement in 1949. Known in the ring as the "Brown Bomber," Louis' boxing career spanned 71 fights, including 25 title defenses.

At the onset of World War II, Louis volunteered for service in the United States Army. He served in both North Africa and Europe where he fought exhibition bouts before Allied troops, eventually appearing before over 2 million soldiers. At the conclusion of the war, TSG Louis was awarded the Legion of Merit for his contributions to the war effort.

Joe Louis died on April 12, 1981. Despite his admirable service, Louis remained ineligible for interment at Arlington because of the stringent burial regulations. However, President Ronald Reagan quickly waived the requirements and authorized Louis' burial at the cemetery.

On April 21st, interdenominational funeral services were conducted for Joe Louis at Arlington National Cemetery. In attendance were fellow heavyweight champions, Muhammad Ali, Joe Frazier, and Joe Walcott, as well as the Reverend Jesse Jackson and Secretary of State Caspar Weinberger. President Reagan, still recuperating from wounds suffered during an assassination attempt, sent a letter to be read at the services. The President's stated:

U.S. Army Photo

Boxing greats Muhammad Ali, Sugar Ray Leonard, and Joe Frazier attend a 1986 memorial service at the grave of Heavyweight Champion Joe Louis.

[I] was privileged and grateful to have had Joe Louis as my friend . . . out of the ring, he was a considerate and soft spoken man. Inside the ring, his courage, strength, and confident skill wrote a unique and unforgettable chapter in sports history. But Joe Louis was more than a sports' legend. His career was an indictment of racial bigotry, and a source of pride and inspiration to millions of white and black people around the world.

The champion's son, Joe Louis Barrow, Jr., eulogized his father:

It's wonderful that we're here at the National Cemetery, where you will finally rest, because you were a patriot, you served the country well, you provided it with the guidance and the faith it needed at a time when the country was down and the people needed a lift . . . You looked at me [during the Vietnam War] and you said 'This is a beautiful country, son, and it's most important that we stand by it. It may make mistakes. It may not be exactly right, but we have to stand by it.' We are going to miss you an awful lot because you were the greatest, truly the greatest.

Joe Louis was buried in Section 7A, just below the Tomb of the Unknown Soldier.

Matthew Henson

Famed Arctic explorer Robert E. Peary was buried with full military honors shortly after his death in 1920. Two years later, the National Geographic Society erected a suitable memorial at the Peary gravesite to commemorate his claim of discovery of the North Pole. The monument was carved from white Maine granite and features a detailed globe with the seven continents in low relief. A bronze star marks the precise location of the North Pole. Inscribed on its base in Latin is the motto, "I will find a way or make one."

During the ensuing years, one of the more frequent visitors to the Peary grave was his longtime friend and collaborator, Matthew Henson. The two originally met in 1887 in a Washington, D.C. clothing store where Henson worked as a stock clerk. Peary initially enlisted Henson for an early expedition to Nicaragua to survey possible sites for a Central American canal.

After their return, Peary began plans for exploring the Arctic in a quest to be the first person to reach the North Pole. Henson would be an integral part of all such expeditions and became an expert dog-sled driver, skilled hunter, and avid explorer. He learned the Eskimo language fluently and because of his dark skin was welcomed by the native inhabitants as a brother. In his 1910 book on the North Pole expeditions, Peary wrote of Henson, "I have taken him with me on each and all of my northern expeditions . . . and almost without exception on each of my 'farthest' sledge trips. This position I have given him, primarily because of his adaptability and fitness for work; secondly on account of his loyalty. He has shared all the physical hardships of my Arctic work. He is now about forty years old, and can handle a sledge better, and is probably a better dog-driver, than any other man living, except some of the best of the Eskimo hunters themselves."

Despite several failed attempts to reach the Pole, Peary and Henson continued to persevere. Together they braved dangerous ice floes, fuel shortages, frigid temperatures, dense fog, and unpredictable Arctic leads until they finally reached their goal on April 6, 1909. Henson was given the honor of placing the Stars and Stripes at the Pole.

When news of their feat finally reached the United States, Peary was hailed as a national hero but Henson received little credit. He eventually moved to Harlem and was forced to accept a menial job in a Bronx garage. Later he became a messenger with the U.S. Customs Service. Efforts to award Henson a pension for his Arctic exploits were

Library of Congress

Arctic Explorer Matthew Henson shortly after being the first African-American to reach the North Pole. Henson placed the American flag at the Pole in 1909 during Robert Peary's expedition.

P. Bigler

The grave of Matthew Henson adjacent to that of his colleague, Robert Peary. Henson was re-interred to Arlington National Cemetery in 1988 in recognition of his status as "Co-discoverer of the North Pole."

consistently thwarted in Congress as was legislation initiated in the 1950's to award him the Medal of Honor. Upon his death in 1955, he was buried in the Woodlawn Cemetery in the Bronx. A small, inconspicuous granite headstone was all that marked his grave, modestly inscribed with the statement, "Reached the North Pole with Peary."

In 1986, Professor Allen Counter of Harvard University began an intensive lobbying campaign to recognize Henson's contributions to Peary's polar expeditions. He requested that Henson's remains be reinterred in Arlington National Cemetery in an area near the Peary gravesite. After several bureaucratic delays, President Ronald Reagan finally granted an exemption from the cemetery's rigorous burial restrictions and authorized Henson's burial at Arlington.

On April 6, 1988, seventy-nine years after reaching the Pole, Henson's remains and those of his wife were buried at Arlington with military honors in a grave adjacent to that of Robert Peary's. A five-foot granite marker was unveiled with an impressive bronze plaque featuring Matthew Henson at the North Pole along with his four Eskimo companions—Egingwah, Ootah, Ooqueah, and Seegloo. The memorial belatedly credits Matthew Henson as the "Co-discoverer of the North Pole."

Terrorism

Americans were the repeated targets of terrorist attacks during the 1980's with United States citizens murdered in Central America, Asia, and the Middle East. The greatest loss of life, however, occurred in Lebanon.

Lebanon, bitterly divided into warring religious factions, threatened the delicate balance of peace in the Middle East. In an effort to bring stability to the region, an international peace mission was established consisting of military contingents from France, Italy, Britain, and the United States. Over 1,600 members of the Eighth Marine Battalion were assigned to the Beirut International Airport but were subjected to constant sniper fire from neighboring communities. On Sunday, October 23rd, 1983, a truck loaded with over 2,000 pounds of explosives crashed through the barricades of the Marine compound and into the barracks of the battalion. The ensuing explosion completely destroyed the building and tragically killed 241 American servicemen, the single largest loss of life of American military personnel since Vietnam. Simultaneously, the French military delegation was similarly bombed sustaining over 50 fatalities.

The vast majority of the young Marines were interred by family members in local cemeteries but 21 of the bombing victims were brought to Arlington National Cemetery to be buried in adjoining graves in Section 59. Subsequently, other victims of terrorism were interred in the same area, including First Lieutenant Dennis Keogh, who was killed in South Africa; Captain George Tsantes, assassinated in Greece; and CIA official Matthew Gannon, killed aboard Pan Am Flight 103 over Lockerbie, Scotland. In 1984, the world's attention was riveted once again on the Middle East when hijackers commandeered a TWA jet and held the passengers and its crew hostage for 17 days. While the plane was in Beirut, the terrorists brutally murdered a Navy diver, SW2 Robert Stethem, and threw his body onto the tarmac. He was later interred in Section 59 near the other victims of terrorist violence. Each week, regardless of the weather or time of year, Stethem's parents continue to decorate Robert's grave with fresh flowers, a silent reminder of the human toll of such insanity.

In 1984, No Greater Love, an organization originally founded to aid the children of soldiers missing or killed in action during the Vietnam war, organized a series of ceremonies to honor the Marines who had died in Lebanon as well as all victims of terrorist activities. On May 1st, 1984, a 14-foot cedar of Lebanon was planted in Section 59 near the graves of the soldiers.

Congress approved a Joint Resolution to set aside the first anniversary of the Beirut bombing as "'A Time of Remembrance,' to urge all Americans to take time to reflect on the sacrifices that have been made in the pursuit of peace and freedom." On October 23rd, 1984, a memorial service was held at Arlington in Section 59 at which time a granite marker at the base of the cedar tree was unveiled. The inscription reads:

"Let Peace Take Root"
This Cedar of Lebanon tree grows in living memory
of the Americans killed in the Beirut terrorist attack
and all victims of terrorism throughout the world.
Dedicated during the first memorial ceremony for
these victims.

Given by No Greater Love

October 23, 1984
A Time of Remembrance

Section 59 has continued to serve as the primary burial location for American military personnel killed during terrorist assaults. However, this is an unofficial designation and other funerals routinely occur in the area.

CHAPTER NINE

Beyond the Stars

—Ronald Reagan

In May 1961, shortly after taking office, President John F. Kennedy responded to a series of Soviet space initiatives by announcing that the United States would undertake a massive effort to land a man on the moon by the end of the decade. In an address delivered before a joint session of Congress, President Kennedy stated: "No single space project in this period will be more impressive to mankind, or more important for the long-range exploration of space . . . in a very real sense, it will not be one man going to the moon . . . it will be an entire nation."

The National Aeronautics and Space Administration (NASA) began a three-tier approach to achieving the President's goal. Beginning with six Mercury flights, the space program was scheduled to progress through a series of two-man Gemini launches and culminate with the lunar-capable Apollo missions.

The Mercury and Gemini flights proved to be stunning successes. A spirit of optimism surrounded the onset of the Apollo project. NASA had assembled an impressive crew for the inaugural flight of *Apollo I*, consisting of three skilled and experienced astronauts, Virgil "Gus" Grissom, Edward White, and Roger "Bruce" Chaffee. The crew commander, Virgil Grissom was the second American in space in 1961, following the flight of Alan Shepard in a similar 15-minute suborbital flight. Grissom's mission was marred, however, by the loss of his capsule, *Liberty Bell "7"*, before recovery efforts could salvage it from the Atlantic. Despite this setback, Grissom served on the first Gemini flight in March 1965, thereby becoming the first American astronaut to serve on two space missions. Assisting Grissom on *Apollo I* was Astronaut Edward White. White had

Astronauts White, Chaffee, and Grissom practice launch procedures aboard Apollo I. *A fire on board the capsule killed all three of the astronauts just four weeks before the scheduled launch.*

also served in the Gemini program and, in June 1965, became the first American to walk in space, leaving his capsule for a 20-minute tethered excursion into space. Roger Chaffee, a Navy test pilot, was the rookie of the mission with the flight of *Apollo I* to be his first venture into space.

Apollo I was scheduled for launch in late February 1967 and was to remain in earth orbit for up to 16 days. On January 27th, just four weeks before the launch date, Grissom, Chaffee, and White entered their Apollo capsule for a series of preflight tests. Five hours into the mock countdown, the crew frantically radioed that there was a fire on board the craft. Members of the attending launchpad crew heroically struggled to free the vessel's hatch, a process requiring a minimum of 90 seconds, but their efforts were hindered by the intensity of the heat fueled by the capsule's pressurized oxygen. Six desperate minutes passed before the hatch finally sprung open but all three astronauts were dead.

President Lyndon Johnson led the nation in mourning the loss of the nation's first space-related fatalities and attended separate funeral ceremonies at Arlington National Cemetery for Chaffee and Grissom. The two astronauts were interred in adjoining graves in Section 3, appropri-

NASA

The flag draped-coffin of Astronaut Gus Grissom is escorted to the grave by fellow space pioneers John Glenn and Alan Shepard.

ately near the grave of another aviation pioneer, Lieutenant Thomas Selfridge. The remains of astronaut Edward White were returned to New York for burial on the grounds of his alma mater, West Point.

Challenger

The Space Shuttle represented a new generation of spacecraft for the United States. For the first time, the space vehicle and many of its component booster parts would be reusable. By 1986, five years after the first successful flight, the shuttle program had been so successful that the flights appeared routine and the major television networks no longer offered live coverage of the launches.

The Space Shuttle *Challenger* was scheduled for its 10th launch on January 22, 1986. Mission 51-L was to last six days and to deploy satellites for improved communications and observation of Halley's Comet. It also included the first private citizen to venture into space, teacher Christa McAuliffe, who had been selected for the flight from over 11,000 applicants. During the mission, she was to deliver a series of live lessons to the nation's school children in what she called "the ultimate field trip."

Unseasonably cold temperatures repeatedly delayed the launch of the *Challenger*. Despite another frigid night, NASA officials agreed to launch on January 28th after consultation with various shuttle contractors. Some 72 seconds into the flight at an altitude of 10 miles, the *Challenger* exploded after a failure of the solid rocket boosters. All seven crew members, Francis "Dick" Scobee, Michael Smith, Judith Resnick, Ellison Onizuka, Ronald McNair, Gregory Jarvis, and Christa McAuliffe, were killed, the first casualties of the space program in 19 years.

Recovery efforts lasted several weeks while Navy and Coast Guard vessels combed the Atlantic seabed searching for debris. Identifiable remains of all the crew members were finally located and the bodies were returned to their families for burial three months after their tragic deaths.

At his family's request, Pilot Michael J. Smith was buried at Arlington National Cemetery with full military honors in Section 7A, just below the Tomb of the Unknown Soldier near the grave of heavyweight champion Joe Louis. His stone bears air wings and a comet, the astronaut's insignia. Two weeks later, Mission Commander, Francis "Dick" Scobee was laid to rest on his forty-seventh birthday, May 19th, in Section 46 adjacent to the grave of the three airmen who lost their lives during the Iranian hos-

U.S. Air Force Photo

Mrs. June Scobee places flowers on the grave of her husband, Space Shuttle Mission Commander Francis "Dick" Scobee. Michael Smith, the pilot of the ill-fated Challenger *was also buried at Arlington.*

tage rescue mission. In an earlier memorial service honoring all of the *Challenger* crew at the Johnson Space Center, President Reagan eulogized: "The nation, too, will long feel the loss of her seven sons and daughters . . . we can find consolation only in faith, for we know in our hearts that you who flew so high and proud now make your home beyond the stars."

On the morning following the Scobee interment, representatives of all seven *Challenger* crew members quietly gathered in Section 46 prior to the normal scheduled opening of the cemetery. In a brief ceremony, an urn containing the ashes of the individually unidentifiable commingled remains of the crew that had also been recovered from the crash site, was placed and sealed into the concrete base of the anticipated *Challenger* memorial. At the behest of the families, the service was conducted without publicity and no acknowledgment of the burial was allowed to be inscribed on the monument to the crew.

The following month, on June 10, 1986, Congress passed a concurrent resolution that stated, "It is the sense of Congress that the Secretary of the Army should construct and place at Arlington National Cemetery a memorial marker honoring the seven members of the crew of the Space Shuttle *Challenger* who died on January 28th, 1986 during the launch of the Space Shuttle Mission 51-L from Cape Canaveral." Although it was hoped that the monument would be ready for dedication on the first anniversary of the tragedy, the ceremony was delayed until March 21, 1987. At that time, Vice President George Bush unveiled and dedicated the granite monument which features a bronze plaque depicting the launch of the space shuttle surrounded by images of its seven crew members. On the back of the memorial is a quotation from the World War II-era poem, "High Flight," written by John Gillespie Magee, which was quoted by President Reagan during his speech to the nation concerning the fate of the *Challenger* crew.

The Persian Gulf War

On August 2, 1990, the world was stunned when Iraq launched a massive invasion of neighboring Kuwait. The small, oil-rich Persian Gulf kingdom was quickly overrun and Saddam Hussein proclaimed it to be Iraq's 19th province.

President George Bush countered by declaring that such naked aggression would not be tolerated and skillfully began to assemble a diverse and powerful military coalition to oppose Hussein. The President immediately ordered American military forces to the region, initiating the largest deployment of the United States armed services since Vietnam. By mid-January, some 514,000 American servicemen and women were in position in Saudi Arabia.

The remains of the barracks of the 476th Quartermaster Corps after it was struck by an Iraqi SCUD missile near the end of the Persian Gulf Conflict. PFC Timothy Shaw was among the 27 killed in the attack and was buried with military honors at Arlington Cemetery.

Despite numerous pronouncements and ultimatums by the United Nations, Hussein steadfastly refused to withdraw from Kuwait. On January 16, 1991, President Bush ordered coalition forces into action. Operation Desert Storm began with a massive air offensive against Baghdad and other Iraqi military targets.

With American military forces fully engaged in combat, Arlington and the nation's other national cemeteries were ordered to stand by to receive casualties. But the air war proved exceptionally efficient and coalition losses were remarkably light. Still, on February 15th, Arlington received its first casualty from the war, Captain Jonathan Edwards, who was killed in action when his AH-1 Cobra helicopter crashed near the Kuwaiti border. That same day, a memorial stone was erected for 1LT Jorge Arteaga whose body was not recovered after his B-52 crashed into the Indian Ocean, apparently shot down by Iraqi defenses.

Because of the scope of the American military commitment, President Bush called up over 40,000 reservists. Most of these troops were utilized in support positions to assist with maintenance, logistics, and supply. The 476th Quartermaster Corps from Greensburg, Pennsylvania, was a military police detachment assigned to duty in Dhahran, Saudi Arabia. On February 25th, as the soldiers were finishing dinner, an Iraqi SCUD missile slammed into their barracks, killing 27 and wounding over 100 others. While most of the casualties were buried in Pennsylvania near the unit's headquarters, PFC Timothy Shaw was buried with military honors at Arlington Cemetery in Section 8.

The Persian Gulf War ended on February 28th with the liberation of Kuwait and the surrender of thousands of Iraqi troops. Still, despite the ceasefire, the military continued to conduct dangerous mine sweeping operations, air patrols, and humanitarian missions. On March 1st, 32-year-old Major Marie Rossi volunteered to fly a mission despite the onset of bad weather. Rossi had gained distinction during the war for her bravery and for having flown into combat. In many ways, she had become a symbol of the ever-expanding role of women in the United States military. On this mission, however, her Chinook helicopter crashed, killing Major Rossi and her crew. She was buried in a grave adjacent to that of PFC Shaw. Her family eulogized, "We are proud as we can be of [Marie's] accomplishments in the service of her country; and we are proud of her bravery, her leadership and her example to others." On Major Rossi's headstone is inscribed, "First Female Combat Commander to Fly in Battle." On the reverse of the monument is a bronze plaque featuring a Chinook helicopter and the fitting sentiment, "May our men and women stand strong and equal."

Eventually, 17 casualties from the Persian Gulf War were buried at Arlington. In addition, nine memorial stones were erected in honor of servicemen who lost their lives and whose remains were unrecoverable.

The Columbarium

Many American veterans were no longer allowed burial at Arlington National Cemetery because of the extensive grave conservation effort and increasingly rigorous eligibility requirements. Yet many of these same servicemen had served with distinction and still desired interment at the cemetery. The Department of the Army in conjunction with the Veterans Administration began to investigate various alternatives to in-ground burial in an effort to accommodate all honorably discharged veterans. Mr. Raymond Costanzo, the superintendent of Arlington, became a leading advocate for a columbarium for cremated remains. He remembers, "The change in the eligibility criteria in the late 60's was very unpopular. There were thousands of veterans that wanted to be buried [at Arlington] and since the new regulations did not permit it, we came up with this concept—the columbarium— whereby cremated remains of veterans could be placed here."

The first structure was formally dedicated in 1980 with a similar building completed in 1985. Two more courts have been added since, with five more additions planned, for a total of 50,000 niches capable of accommodating 100,000 remains. Mr. Costanzo believes that the columbarium has proven to be a successful addition to the cemetery, "We anticipated about 700 [inurnments] per year. It's running well

R. Cramer

The Columbarium for cremated remains opened in 1980. Eventually nine such structures are planned.

over 1,000 per year and growing steadily. It's something I think is good for the veterans."

The Women in Military Service Memorial

The Arlington Memorial Archway was originally intended to provide a grand entrance into the cemetery. Commissioned during the Great Depression, the structure was never completely finished and failed to achieve its intended purpose.

In the mid-1980's, General Wilma Vaught (USAF-ret) and members of the Women in Military Service Foundation, secured permission from the National Capitol Memorial Commission to use the archway as part of a monument to honor the 1.8 million women who had served in the Armed Services. A design competition was held and in November 1989, the project was awarded to architects Marion Weiss and Michael Manfiedi.

The initial design incorporated an innovative use of skylights, prisms, and glass spires that would provide a soft glow at night. The National Capitol Memorial Commission, however, feared that such a design was incompatible with the Kennedy gravesite and required substantial modifications to ensure the integrity of the eternal flame.

After the final plans were approved, construction of the new memorial began on June 22, 1995. The finished monument was formally dedicated during a four-day celebration in October 1997. The Women in Military Service Memorial houses a theater, an exhibit area, and a computerized register of women veterans. It serves to recognize the contributions and honorable service that women have historically provided to the United States both in peacetime and at war.

The Future of Arlington

For over two decades, despite Arlington's increasing number of visitors, two small trailers served as the cemetery's visitor's center. Although these structures were intended to be temporary, government budget constraints prevented the replacement of the inadequate facilities until 1986 when ground was finally broken for a new, $8 million complex. The new building was formally opened in 1988 and now provides tourist and visitors to the cemetery an appropriate orientation to Arlington. The building features an impressive display of mural-size photographs documenting many of the important events in the cemetery's history along with a grave information counter and a book store. Display cases are located throughout the building, including one that exhibits Arlington's first burial register opened to the page where Pvt. William H. Christman's name is inscribed. Tickets are likewise available for tourist transportation throughout the cemetery grounds

R. Cramer

The rows of endless headstones bear silent testimony to the nation's military heroes.

and there are plans to eventually relocate the cemetery's historian's office to the building. Superintendent Raymond Costanzo, who was a determined advocate for the Visitors Center, believes that the building is ". . . a place where the visitors can be well received in a quality atmosphere." Furthermore, he feels that tourist will be able to ". . . get a brief orientation of what the cemetery's all about and then visually enjoy it."

In December, 1990, Ray Costanzo retired after 18 years of distinguished service. On January 14, 1991, in the midst of the Persian Gulf conflict, John C. Metzler assumed the superintendent's duties. Metzler, the son of a former Arlington chief, had grown up on the cemetery's grounds and had witnessed many of its most historic moments, including the funerals of John and Robert Kennedy. During the Vietnam War, he served as a helicopter crew chief and later became the director of several national cemeteries. Under his current leadership, Arlington has begun to prepare for the next century when space limitations will greatly threaten its continued operation as an active military cemetery.

Arlington completed its 230,000th burial in 1993. With less than 50,000 vacant graves remaining, combined with the anticipated expansion of the columbarium, Arlington is still expected to remain an active cemetery for at least another 30 years, after which time it will be maintained as a national shrine. Historically, however, whenever Arlington has been in danger of closing, additional land has been obtained, allowing for expansion or the cemetery's regulations were modified to ensure its continued operation. Former superintendent Raymond Costanzo believes that similar efforts will be made in the future. He maintains, "I fully expect that sometime around the turn of the century, someone is going to begin to look very seriously at the impact of closing Arlington. I think you'll see some adjustments made in boundaries . . . where additional land will be made available."

Arlington National Cemetery will certainly continue to operate well into the next century. During that time, the world's attention will periodically focus again on the nation's burial ground. The greatest future for Arlington was envisioned by President John F. Kennedy a quarter of a century ago when he foresaw a time when " . . . there will be no veterans of any further wars . . . because all shall have learned to live together in peace." When that time comes, perhaps those who will continue to be buried at Arlington will be remembered not for how they died, but for the contributions they made while living. Meanwhile, the countless headstones at Arlington National Cemetery serve as a silent reminder of the valor of those American servicemen and women who eternally rest . . . *in honored glory.*

Appendix A
Notable Names and
Burial Locations

NAME	SEC.	GRAVE
Arnold, Henry *Gen. of the Army*	34	44-A
Batista, Marlo *Italian POW*	15C	347-4
Berger, Warren *Chief Justice*	5	7015-2
Boyington, Pappy *Col.*	7A	176
Bradley, Omar *Gen. of the Army*	30	428-1&2
Brown, Ron *Sec. of Commerce*	6	8389-B
Bryan, William Jennings	4	3118
Chaffee, Roger Bruce *Astronaut*	3	2502-F
Chennault, Clair *Lt. Gen.*	2	873-4
Christman, William Henry *Pvt.*	27	19
Commerford, John *Superintendent*	1	545-WS
Doolittle, Jimmy *Gen.*	7A	111
Doubleday, Abner *Gen.*	1	61
Dulles, John Foster *Sec. of State*	21	S-31
Evers, Medgar *Civil Rights Advocate*	36	1431
Gagnon, Rene *Cpl.*	51	543
Grissom, Virgil *Astronaut*	3	2503-F
Halsey, William *Fleet Admiral*	2	1184
Hayes, Ira *Cpl.*	34	479-A
Henson, Matthew *Arctic Explorer*	8	LOT S-15
Hilberath, Anton *German POW*	15C	347-1
Holmes, Oliver Wendell *Justice*	5	LOT 7004-A
Hopper, Grace Murray *Rear Admiral*	59	973
Irwin, James *Astronaut*	3	2503-G-2
Kearny, Philip *Gen.*	2	LOT S-8
L'Enfant, Pierre	2	LOT 3
Lansdowne, Zachary *LCDR*	4	3122
Leahy, William *Fleet Admiral*	2	932
Lincoln, Robert Todd	31	LOT 13
Lingan, James McCubbin *Gen.*	1	LOT 299
Louis, Joe *Heavyweight Champion*	7A	177
MacArthur, Arthur *Gen.*	2	879

Marshall, George C. *Gen. of the Army*	7	LOT 8198
Marshall, Thurgood *Justice*	5	40-3
Marvin, Lee *Actor*	7A	176
McAuliffe, Anthony *Gen.*	3	2536
Meigs, Montgomery *Gen.*	1	LOT 1
Metzler, John J. *Superintendent*	7A	86
Mitchell, John *Attorney General*	7A	121
Murphy, Audie *Major*	46	366-11
Muskie, Edmund *Senator*	6	8724-A
Parks, James *Former Custis Slave*	15	152
Peary, Robert *Rear Admiral*	8	LOT S-15
Pershing, John J. *Gen. of the Armies*	34	S-19
Powers, Francis Gary *U-2 Pilot*	11	658-2
Prudenza, Archangelo *Italian POW*	15C	347-4
Randolph, Wallace Fitz *Gen.*	1	132
Reed, Walter *Major*	3	LOT 1864
Reynolds, Frank *Journalist*	7A	180
Rich, Lorimer *Architect*	48	288
Rickover, Hyman *Admiral*	5	7000
Ridgeway, Matthew *General*	7	8196-1
Robinson, Roscoe *General*	7A	18
Rosecrans, William Starke *MG.*	3	1862
Rossi, Marie Therese *Major*	8	9872
Scobee, Francis *Astronaut*	46	1129-3
Selfridge, Thomas *Lt*	3	2158
Sheridan, Philip *Gen.*	2	LOT 1
Sickles, Daniel *MG.*	3	1906-WS
Smith, Bedell *General*	7	8197-A
Smith, Michael *Astronaut*	7A	208-1
Strank, Michael *Sgt.*	12	7179
Stetham, Robert *SW2-DV*	59	430
Stewart, Potter *Justice*	5	40-2
Taft, William Howard *President*	30	S-14
Tanner, James *Cpl.*	2	877
Taylor, Maxwell *Gen.*	7A	20
Van Fleet, James A. *Gen.*	7	8195-A
Wainwright, Jonathan *Gen.*	1	358-B
Warren, Earl *Chief Justice*	21	S-32
Younger, Edward F. *Sgt.*	18	1918

Monuments, Cenotaphs, and Group Burials

NAME	SEC.	GRAVE
Argonne Cross	18	
Army and Navy Nurses Monument	21	
Canadian Cross	46	
Cedar of Lebanon	59	
Challenger Memorial	46	
Chaplains Monument	2E	
Coast Guard Memorial	4	
Confederate Memorial	16	
Experimental Stone	13	13615
U.S.S. Forrestal	46	556-7-8
Iranian Hostage Rescue Mission	46	1124-3
U.S.S. Liberty	34	1817
Mast of the *U.S.S. Maine*	24	
Miller, Glenn *Major*	MH	464-A
Pan Am 103	1	
Rough Riders Memorial	22	
Serpens Memorial	34	
Spanish-American War Memorial	22	
2,111 Unknowns	26	
War of 1812 Unknowns	1	298

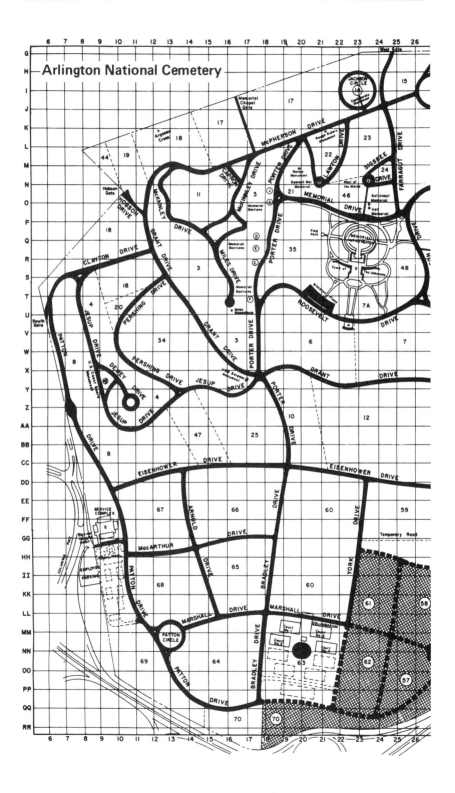

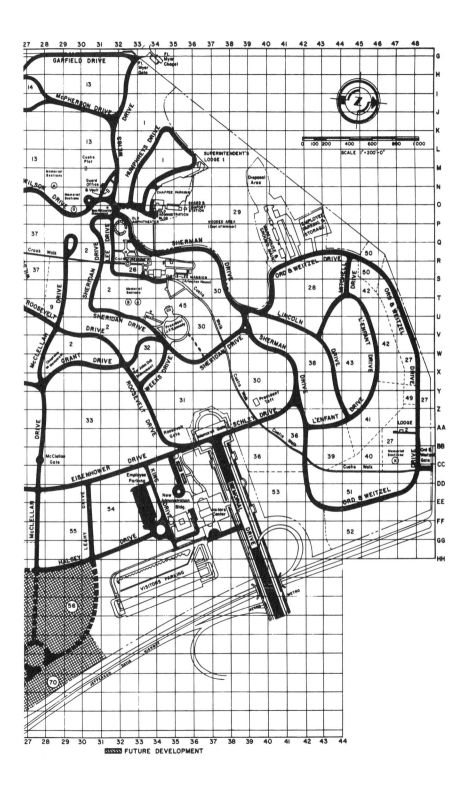

APPENDIX B
ARLINGTON CHRONOLOGY

1608   Captain John Smith explores the upper Potomac River in the vicinity of Arlington.

1669   Robert Howsing receives a six thousand acre land grant from Governor Berkeley of Virginia.

1778   John Parke Custis, the son of Martha Washington, purchases the eleven hundred acre Arlington tract.

1781   After the Battle of Yorktown, John Parke Custis dies from illness.

1802   The construction of Arlington House begins.

1804   George Washington Parke Custis marries Mary Lee Fitzhugh.

1824   The Marquis de Lafayette visits the Arlington estate while on a grand tour of the United States.

1831   Mary Custis weds Robert E. Lee at Arlington House.

1857   George Washington Parke Custis dies and entails the land to his daughter, Mary Custis Lee.

1861   Robert E. Lee leaves Arlington to join the Virginia state militia; Union troops cross the Potomac and occupy the estate.

1862   Congress passes "An Act for the Collection of Taxes in Insurrectionary Districts."

1864   William H. Christman and William H. McKinney are the first soldiers buried on the Arlington estate; the cemetery is formally commissioned.

1866   2,111 unknowns are buried in a crypt near the Arlington mansion.

1868   General Logan issues Order #11 creating "Decoration Day."

1870   Robert E. Lee dies in Lexington, Virginia.

1872   Regulations require the use of uniform stones in enlisted areas.

1873   Mary Custis Lee visits her old Arlington home; she dies five months later and is buried along side her husband in Lexington, Virginia.

1874   The "old" Amphitheater is dedicated near the Arlington House mansion.

1882   The United States Supreme Court declares the federal government a trespasser and orders the estate returned to its antebellum condition.

1883   Custis Lee sells Arlington to the federal government for $150,000.

1888   Memorial Day is declared a national holiday.

1889   Arlington annexes 142 acres of land.

1892   The first Revolutionary War dead are reinterred to Arlington.

1897   Arlington annexes 56 acres of land.

1899   The first Spanish-American War casualties are buried in the cemetery, the first time that American soldiers are returned from foreign soil for interment.

1902   The Spanish-American War Memorial is dedicated.

1903   Arlington burials reach 19,000; 300 funerals are being conducted annually.

1905   Fourteen Unknowns from the War of 1812 are buried in Section 1.

1908   Lt. Thomas Selfridge, the first casualty of powered flight, is buried at Arlington after the crash of a plane piloted by Orville Wright.

1909   Pierre L'Enfant, the designer of the city of Washington, D.C., is buried in front of Arlington House on a ridge overlooking the nation's capital.

1915   Construction of the Memorial Amphitheater begins; Woodrow Wilson lays the corner stone.

1920   The Memorial Amphitheater is dedicated.

1921   The World War I Unknown Soldier is buried on the plaza of the Amphitheater.

1925   Restoration of the Arlington House mansion is begun.

1926   Robert Todd Lincoln, the son of President Abraham Lincoln, is interred at Arlington Cemetery on a hill overlooking the Lincoln Memorial.

1930   Former President and Chief Justice of the Supreme Court, William Howard Taft, becomes the first chief executive buried at Arlington.

1932 The cap-stone to the Tomb of the Unknown Soldier is completed, bringing the Tomb to its present shape; the Memorial Bridge connecting Arlington to Washington, D.C. is completed.

1933 Arlington House is transferred to the jurisdiction of the National Park Service.

1937 The Tomb of the Unknown Soldier is placed under a twenty-four hour honor guard; the Memorial Gateway is dedicated providing the western terminus to Memorial Bridge.

1940 At year's end, 49,927 Americans have been buried at Arlington Cemetery.

1941 Ignace Paderewski is allowed temporary repose in the Mast of the *U.S.S. Maine* Memorial.

1944 Manuel Quezon of the Philippines also is allowed temporary repose in the Mast of the *U.S.S. Maine* Memorial until his nation is liberated from the Japanese.

1945 The first World War II prisoners of war are buried at Arlington in accordance with the Geneva Convention.

1948 General of the Armies John J. "Black Jack" Pershing, the former commander of the American Expeditionary Forces, is buried.

1950 Over 70,000 American soldiers and servicemen have been interred at Arlington.

1955 Arlington House is designated a memorial to General Robert E. Lee.

1958 The double interment ceremonies for the World War II and Korean War Unknowns are held at the Memorial Amphitheater.

1959 The 100,000th burial takes place at Arlington in April.

1962 The policy of accepting grave reservations ends at Arlington and all national cemeteries.

1963 President John Fitzgerald Kennedy is buried at Arlington after his assassination in Dallas, Texas.

1966 During peak months, daily visitation at the cemetery reaches 50,000; Fort Myer South Post is annexed by Arlington bringing the cemetery to its current 612 acres.

1967   Two of the three *Apollo I* astronauts are interred after a launch pad fire; the John F. Kennedy memorial grave is dedicated; victims of the *U.S.S. Forrestal* fire are buried in Section 46.

1968   Senator Robert F. Kennedy is buried after his assassination.

1969   The Archbishop of Krakow, Karol Wojtyla, the future Pope John-Paul II, visits Arlington and views the coffin of Ignace Paderewski.

1970   Arlington is closed to vehicular traffic.

1971   Audie Murphy, the most decorated American soldier in World War II, is buried after his death in a plane crash; the Robert F. Kennedy gravesite is completed.

1976   Medal of Honor headstones are highlighted with gold lettering; the Historian's Office is created; Queen Elizabeth of England, King Juan Carlos of Spain, and Emperor Hirohito of Japan visit Arlington during the nation's bicentennial celebrations.

1977   Francis Gary Powers, the U-2 pilot shot down over the Soviet Union in 1960, is buried after his death in a helicopter crash.

1980   Three airmen from the aborted Iranian hostage rescue mission are laid to rest; the Columbarium for cremated remains is opened.

1981   General of the Army Omar Bradley, the last of the five star generals, is buried after a state funeral.

1983   Twenty-one soldiers killed in a terrorist bombing in Beirut, Lebanon, are interred in Section 59.

1984   The Vietnam Unknown Serviceman is interred at the Tomb of the Unknown Soldier.

1986   Dick Scobee and Michael Smith, two members of the crew of the Space Shuttle *Challenger* are buried; construction on a new visitors center is begun; Arlington completes its 200,000th burial.

1987   The *Challenger* memorial is dedicated in Section 46.

1988   The remains of Polar explorer Matthew Henson is reinterred to Arlington; the new visitors center is dedicated.

1989   Michael Gannon, one of the victims of the terrorist bombing of Pan Am Flight 103, is buried in Section 59; six of the sailors killed after a turret explosion on the *U.S.S. Iowa* are interred at Arlington.

1991   Seventeen casualties from the Persian Gulf War are buried at Arlington; nine memorial stones are erected for other military personnel whose remains were not recovered.

1992   Ignace Jan Paderewski is returned to his native Poland fifty-one years after his death.

1993   Former Justice and civil rights activist, Thurgood Marshall, is buried in Section 5; General Matthew Ridgeway, the American commander of the Eighth Army in Korea, is interred; Arlington completes its 230,000th burial.

1994   Jacqueline Kennedy Onassis is interred; a memorial service is held to commemorate the 50th anniversary of the Normandy invasion.

1995   Ground breaking for the Women in Military Service Memorial; Chief Justice Warren Burger is buried; the Pan Am 103 Memorial is dedicated in Section 1.

1996   Sgt. Heather Johnsen becomes the first female badge holder.

1998   Vietnam Unknown is exhumed and later identified as Captain Michael Blassey.

Appendix C
John F. Kennedy Gravesite:
Inscriptions

Let the word go forth
From this time and place
To friend and foe alike
That the torch has been passed
To a new generation of Americans

Let every nation know
Whether it wishes us well or ill
That we shall pay any price—bear any burden
Meet any hardship—support any friend
Oppose any foe to assure the survival
And the success of liberty

Now the trumpet summons us again
Not as a call to bear arms—though embattled we are
But a call to bear the burden of a long twilight struggle
A struggle against the common enemies of man
Tyranny—Poverty—Disease—and War itself

In the long history of the world
Only a few generations have been granted
The role of defending freedom
In the hour of maximum danger
I do not shrink from this responsibility
I welcome it

The Energy—the Faith—The Devotion
Which we bring to this endeavor
Will light our country
And all who serve it
And the glow from that fire
Can truly light the world

And so my fellow Americans
Ask not what your country can do for you

Ask what you can do for your country
My fellow citizens of the world—ask not
What America will do for you—but what together
We can do for the freedom of man

With a good conscience our only sure reward
With history the final judge of our deeds
Let us go forth to lead the land we love—asking His blessing
And his help—but knowing that here on earth
God's work must truly be our own

Inaugural Address—January 20, 1961

Robert F. Kennedy Gravesite Inscriptions

It is from numberless diverse acts of courage and belief that human history is shaped. Each time a man stands up for an ideal, or acts to improve the lot of others, or strikes out against injustice, he sends forth a tiny ripple of hope, and crossing each other from a million different centers of energy and daring, those ripples build a current that can sweep down the mightiest walls of oppression and resistance.

South Africa, 1966

Aeschylus wrote: "In our sleep, pain that cannot forget falls drop by drop upon the heart and in our despair, against our will comes wisdom through the awful grace of God."

What we need in the United States is not division, what we need in the United States is not hatred, what we need in the United States is not violence or lawlessness, but love and wisdom and compassion toward one another, and a feeling of justice toward those who still suffer within our country, whether they be white or they be black. Let us dedicate ourselves to what the Greeks wrote so many years ago: to tame the savageness of man and make gentle the life of this world. Let us dedicate ourselves to that and say a prayer for our country and people.

Indianapolis, 1968

National Archives

The grave of Senator Robert F. Kennedy on June 9th, 1969, the day following his funeral at Arlington. Flowers mark the location of the burial near his brother's grave. In 1971, the current I.M. Pei designed gravesite was dedicated.

APPENDIX D
ELIGIBILITY

The following eligibility requirements have been excerpted from pamphlets available from the Department of the Army.

Interment requirements at Arlington National Cemetery

Because space is limited, burial at Arlington National Cemetery is restricted to a very few categories of those who have served honorably in the Armed Forces. These include:

1. Those who have died on active duty.
2. Those having at least 20 years active duty or active reserve service which qualifies them for retired pay either upon retirement or at age 60, and those retired for disability.
3. Veterans honorably discharged for 30% (or more) disability before 1 October 1949.
4. Holders of the Nation's highest military decorations (Medal of Honor; Distinguished Service Cross, Air Force Cross or Navy Cross; Distinguished Service Medal; and Silver Star) or the Purple Heart.
5. The spouse or unmarried minor (under 21) child of any of the above or of any person already buried in Arlington. An unmarried dependent student qualifies up to age 23.
6. An unmarried adult child with physical or mental disability acquired before age 21.
7. Provided certain special requirements are met, a veteran who is the parent, brother, sister or child of an eligible person already interred. Interment must be in the same grave as the primary eligible, the veteran's spouse must waive his or her eligibility for Arlington, and the veteran can have no dependent children at the time of death.

Those Not Eligible

1. Except as indicated above, parents, brothers, sisters, or in-laws are not eligible, even if they are dependents of an eligible person. Neither is the remarried widow or widower of an eligible person, unless the former is no longer married at death. A person whose last discharge was less-than-honorable is also ineligible.

Inurnment Requirements at Arlington

In April of 1980, the first 5,000-niche section of Arlington National Cemetery's Columbarium for cremated remains was opened for use. Eventually, 50,000 niches will be provided. The Columbarium is located in the southeast section of the Cemetery about half a mile from the Memorial Gate.

1. Any member of the Armed Forces who dies on active duty.

2. Any former member of the Armed Forces who served on active duty (other than for training) and whose last service ended honorably.

3. Certain reservists and ROTC members who die while on active duty; while training or on authorized travel, or while hospitalized as the result of active duty, training, or authorized travel.

4. American members of allied forces whose last service ended honorably.

5. Certain commissioned officers of the U.S. Coast and Geodetic Survey (National Oceanic and Atmospheric Administration) or of the U.S. Public Health Service.

6. The spouse or unmarried minor or permanently dependent child of any of the above, or of any person already in the Columbarium. A student qualifies up to age 23.

Those Not Eligible

1. Parents, brothers, sisters or in-laws—even if they live with, or are dependents of, an eligible person.

2. A person whose last separation from the Armed Forces was under less-than-honorable conditions, even though he or she may receive veteran's benefits.

3. A person who has volunteered for the Armed Forces but has not entered upon active duty.

4. A remarried former spouse of a deceased service member (unless the remarriage is terminated by divorce from or death of the second spouse).

Arlington does not accept grave reservations. Further information may be obtained by writing: The Superintendent, Arlington National Cemetery, Arlington, Virginia 22211.

Headstone Symbols

In the newer areas of the Cemetery, only government headstones are permitted in order to maintain the uniform appearance of the sections. If an individual wishes a private marker, the grave must be located in an area that has such monuments. Private markers are provided at family expense but government headstones are supplied free of charge from the Veterans Administration. Only government niche covers are permitted in the Columbarium. Family members may choose a religious or philosophical emblem from an approved list of 26 such symbols.

1. Christian/Latin Cross
2. Wheel of Righteousness
3. Star of David (Jewish)
4. Presbyterian
5. Russian Orthodox
6. Lutheran
7. Episcopal
8. Unitarian
9. United Methodist
10. Aaronic Order
11. Mormon—Angel Moroni
12. Native American
13. Serbian Orthodox
14. Bahai
15. Atheist
16. Muslim
17. Hindu
18. Greek
19. Konko-Kyo Faith
20. Reorganized Church of Latter Day Saints
21. Sufishm Reoriented
22. Tenrikyo
23. Seicho-No-Ie
24. World Messianity (Izunome)
25. United Church of Religious Science
26. Christian Reformed Church

APPENDIX E
21 FACTS ABOUT ARLINGTON CEMETERY

1. Flags located in the cemetery are lowered to half-staff thirty minutes before the first burial and remain lowered until after the last funeral is completed. Flags are flown at full-staff at all other times except during periods of official mourning and on certain national holidays.

2. President John F. Kennedy made three official visits to Arlington while in office, the last on Veterans' Day, 1963, just eleven days before his assassination.

3. Mrs. Jacqueline Kennedy and Attorney General Robert F. Kennedy placed several items in the President's casket prior to burial. These include three letters, a pair of cuff links, a piece of scrimshaw engraved with the presidential seal, a silver rosary, and a PT-109 tie clasp.

4. Arlington is the only national cemetery authorized to use horses and caissons as a regular part of its funeral ceremonies. The caisson used during the funerals of Presidents Franklin D. Roosevelt and John F. Kennedy is still in daily operation.

5. The original funeral architecture from the first Kennedy gravesite is now held in storage in Boston, Massachusetts.

6. Every American president since Woodrow Wilson has visited Arlington National Cemetery at least once while in office.

7. The first national cemetery was created in 1862 at the behest of President Abraham Lincoln " . . . for the soldiers who shall die in the service of their country." Fourteen cemeteries were created in that year for the dead from the Civil War. Arlington was established in 1864. By 1871, the remains of 300,000 Union soldiers were buried in national cemeteries with approximately 42% individually unidentified.

8. There are currently 115 national cemeteries in 39 states and Puerto Rico, providing graves for over two million American veterans. Seventy-three of the cemeteries were created during and immediately after the American Civil War. Of the 300,000 soldiers interred from that conflict, fully 50% were unknown. Arlington is

the best known of the national cemeteries. The largest in terms of acreage is the Calverton National Cemetery in New York consisting of over 902 acres. The Long Island National Cemetery has the most burials with well over 300,000 interments. The Tahoma National Cemetery in Washington is the newest of the national cemeteries and was dedicated in 1997. Four additional cemeteries are scheduled to open in 1999 to accommodate the increased need for grave space.

9. Over 2,000 ceremonies are conducted at the Tomb of the Unknown Soldier annually. Foreign heads of state and dignitaries regularly place a wreath at the Tomb to honor all American veterans. During state visits, honor guard contingents from all of the Armed Services participate during the ceremonies at the Tomb.

10. Arlington currently averages 25 funerals per day, approximately 6,200 annually. The cemetery has less than 50,000 vacant graves and is expected to reach its capacity around the year 2025 after which it will continue to operate as a national shrine.

11. There are 4,735 unknowns buried at Arlington, the vast majority from the Civil War. During that conflict, a soldier killed in action had a one in three chance of not being identified.

12. During the Memorial Day weekend, individual American flags are placed on all the graves by members of the 3d Infantry. The flags remain in place until after the conclusion of the Memorial Day ceremonies.

13. There are two American presidents buried at Arlington—John F. Kennedy and William Howard Taft. Taft holds the distinction of being the only person to have been both President and Chief Justice of the Supreme Court.

14. Three of the six Iwo Jima flag-raisers are interred at Arlington— Ira Hayes, Michael Strank, and Rene Gagnon.

15. Dead from every American War from the Revolution through the Persian Gulf conflict are buried at Arlington. Pre-1864 dead were reinterred after the cemetery began operations.

16. Five of the nine World War II five-star generals and admirals are buried at Arlington—Halsey, Marshall, Leahy, Arnold, and Bradley.

17. There are two mausoleums—the Miles and Sullivan—located in the cemetery. Above ground interments are no longer permitted.

18. Arlington House was converted into a monument to Robert E. Lee by act of Congress in 1955 and is administered by the National Park Service.

19. Arlington is the only national cemetery operated by the United States Army. All other cemeteries fall under the jurisdiction of the Veterans' Administration.

20. Forty-four foreign nationals from ten countries are buried at Arlington. Most were associated with embassies during war-time and died in the United States which entitled them to burial in a national cemetery. One German and two Italian prisoners-of-war were interred in accordance with the Geneva Convention which entitled captured soldiers to burial with military honors.

21. Over 3,800 former slaves are buried at Arlington. Most fled to Washington during the Civil War to escape bondage, while others lived in the Freedmen's Village that housed some 1,100 blacks after the war. The Village was located near the site of the present Memorial Amphitheater.

APPENDIX F
THE CAISSON PLATOON

One of the most memorable sights at Arlington National Cemetery is the full honor funeral in which the flag-draped casket of the deceased is solemnly borne to the gravesite on top of a horse-drawn caisson. Like most American military funeral customs, this tradition had its origins during the Civil War. At that time, an army's artillery required massive support to sustain it during battle, so each gun was assigned a caisson for supply. These vehicles actually consisted of two tandem pieces—the limber, which was used to store additional ammunition and the caisson itself, which was a flat-bed wagon stocked with feed for the horses, additional supplies, extra rations, and even a spare wheel. The caissons were usually pulled by a generous allotment of six horses, all individually saddled and in-harness so that they could be quickly deployed to replace those animals killed or wounded in battle. Likewise, when their supplies were removed, the caissons proved to be convenient ambulances to remove the battlefield wounded to the regiment's hospital or to cart off the dead for burial.

P. Bigler

Members of the caisson platoon harness the swing team in preparation for a full-honor funeral. Arlington is the only American cemetery that continues to use horses as a regular part of its funeral services.

Arlington is the only national cemetery that continues to use horse-drawn caissons as a routine part of its military funerals. Full honor funerals are conducted on average twice per day but the Caisson Platoon, Co. H, 3d U.S. Infantry (the Old Guard), can accommodate up to six such burials.

There are thirty-three men assigned to the outfit—one warrant officer and thirty-two enlisted men. 1Sgt. Michael Wilson is the sergeant currently in charge of the platoon. All of the men are volunteers and have been recruited from the ranks of the 3d Infantry because of their outstanding service records and their desire to work with horses. Three of the soldiers are experts in leather repair and are responsible for making and maintaining all of the tack and harnesses used by the platoon. One soldier is a trained veterinary technician and another is an animal care specialist. The remainder of the soldiers are Army infantrymen.

When a soldier is first assigned to caisson duty, he undergoes three months of rigorous training before ever participating in a military funeral. During that time, he is expected to learn the anatomy of a horse and is instructed on how to detect and identify symptoms of disease. He is also taught how to ride both in-saddle and bareback on a variety of horses since each animal has a distinct personality and temperament. After the soldier is deemed competent, he is then trained to control two horses in-harness simultaneously. Only after these skills have been completely mastered, will the soldier be placed into funeral rotation as the lead rider. He is responsible for the caisson's front two horses (the lead team) which are generally the smallest and easiest to control animals. After six months of service, a soldier then advances to the middle pair of horses, the swing team. Finally, after nine months with the Caisson Platoon, he is assigned the wheel team, the most powerful and important horses since they are primarily responsible for stopping the caisson.

There are two caissons in daily use at Arlington Cemetery. Both were built in 1918 by the American Carriage and Foundry Co. to support 75 mm. artillery pieces. These caissons, however, were quickly made obsolete by mechanized warfare during World War I and were scrapped, only to be salvaged for use at the cemetery.

The stables are located on post at Fort Myer and house thirty-eight horses—twenty black, seventeen gray, and a foal which was born in May, 1992. They are teamed according to color and are alternated each week. The stables are equipped with a fully operational blacksmith shop run by Peter Cote, the only practicing blacksmith still employed by the United States military. He is responsible for shoeing all of the animals, a procedure that each horse requires every six weeks.

Preparation for a full honor funeral takes fully five hours. The soldiers assigned duty that day report to the stables each morning at 0400 hours. They must first pull the selected horses from their stalls, pick their hooves, and check their shoes. The animals then must be carefully trimmed, groomed, and washed. All of the tack must be prepared, brass polished, and the McClellan saddles shined. Once these duties are completed, the horses are ready to be tacked up. The soldiers finally change into their dress Army uniforms complete with boots and spurs. Finally, the horses are bridled and hooked up to the caisson. After the soldiers saddle up, the section sergeant, who rides his own mount independent of the caisson, reads their orders and the funeral is finally conducted with appropriate ceremony and dignity.

Caparison Horse

For infantry officers of colonel rank and above, a caparison or riderless horse, follows the caisson to the gravesite. The black horse, the solemn color of mourning, has a sword strapped to its English riding saddle with boots reversed in the stirrups. The unmounted horse symbolizes the fact that the soldier will never ride again to lead his troops.

John F. Kennedy Library

"Black Jack" at the U.S. Capitol on November 25th, 1963. The McClellan saddle is equipped with a sword and boots reversed in the stirrups to signify a fallen leader.

There are currently three caparison horses—Palo Alto, Appomattox, and Maddy. They are never harnessed to a caisson but often will serve additional duty as the section sergeant's mount. Although the custom of a riderless horse can be traced to ancient cultures, the first notable use of a caparison horse in the United States occurred during the funeral of President Abraham Lincoln. During the final funeral procession in Springfield, Illinois, Lincoln's personal mount, Old Bob, was led behind the assassinated President's casket to the gravesite at the Oak Ridge Cemetery. The custom was later adopted by the armed services and expanded to include other high ranking military officers.

The most notable recent use of a caparison horse was during the funeral of President John F. Kennedy. Black Jack, a spry and skittish animal, captured the nation's attention and seemed to epitomize the youth and vigor of the slain President. Black Jack was the last of the horses commissioned by the Quartermaster Corps and served as a caparison horse in many other important funerals including those of Dwight D. Eisenhower, Douglas MacArthur, and Lyndon Johnson. Black Jack died at Fort Myer in 1976 at the advanced age of 29 and was buried on the post's parade grounds. The caisson platoon has since converted Black Jack's original stall into a museum honoring his historic service to the nation.

SELECTED BIBLIOGRAPHY

Much of the material used in the preparation of this book comes from the files at the Historian's Office at Arlington National Cemetery and the record groups of the National Archives.

Above and Beyond: A History of the Medal of Honor from the Civil War to Vietnam. Boston: Boston Publishing Company, 1985.

Avil, Howard. *United States National Military Cemetery: Arlington Virginia.* Washington, D.C.: Levin C. Handy, 1903.

Connelly, Thomas L. *The Marble Man: Robert E. Lee and His Image in American Society.* Baton Rouge: Louisiana State University Press, 1977.

Costanzo, Raymond. Personal Interview. 25 August 1986.

Counter, S. Allen. *North Pole Legacy: Black, White, and Eskimo.* Amherst: University of Massachusetts Press, 1991.

Dolan, Edward F. *Matthew Henson: Black Explorer.* New York: Dodd, Mead & Company, 1979.

Flood, Charles Bracelen. *Lee: The Last Years.* Boston: Houghton Mifflin Co., 1981.

Forbes-Lindsay, C. H. *Washington: The City and Seat of Government.* Philadelphia: John C. Winston, Co., 1908.

Four Days. comp. by United Press International and American Heritage Magazine. New York: Simon and Schuster, 1964.

Freeman, Douglas Southall. *Robert E. Lee: A Biography.* New York: Charles Scribner's Sons, 1940.

Fuqua, Paul. Telephone Interview. 15 August 1986.

Hinkel, John Vincent. *Arlington: Monuments to Heroes.* Englewood Cliffs: Prentice-Hall, Inc., 1970.

Johnson, Lyndon. *The Vantage Point: Perspectives on the Presidency, 1963-1969.* New York: Holt, Rinehart and Winston, 1971.

Kavenaugh, James. "A Visit to the Grave." *Catholic Digest,* July 1965, pp. 8-11.

MacDonald, Rose. *Mrs. Robert E. Lee.* Boston: Ginn and Company, 1939.

Mack, William P. and Royal W. Connell. *Naval Ceremonies, Customs, and Traditions*. Annapolis: Naval Institute Press, 1986.

Manchester, William. *The Death of a President*. New York: Harper & Row, 1967.

Mose, James A. *Origin and Significance of Military Customs: Including Military Miscellany of Interest to Soldiers and Civilians*. Menasha: George Banta Publishing Company, 1917.

Moseman, B.C. and M.W. Stark. *The Last Salute: Civil and Military Funerals, 1921-1969*. Washington, D.C.: GPO, 1971.

"The National Geographic Society's Memorial to Peary," *National Geographic Magazine*, June 1922, pp. 639-646.

Nelligan, Murray H. "'Old Arlington': The Story of the Lee Mansion National Memorial." Unpublished manuscript. National Park Service, 1953.

Peary, Robert E. *The North Pole: Its Discovery in 1909 Under the Auspices of the Peary Arctic Club*. New York: Frederick A. Stokes, 1910.

Powers, Dave. Personal Interview. 6 August 1986.

Robertson, James. Personal Interview. 24 June 1986.

Rose, C.B. *Arlington County Virginia: A History*. Baltimore: Port City Press, 1976.

Ross, Bill. *Iwo Jima: Legacy of Valor*. New York: Vantage Press, 1986.

Schildt, Roberta. "Freedman's Village: Arlington, Virginia, 1863-1900," *The Arlington Historical Magazine*, 7 October 1984, pp. 11-21.

Templeman, Eleanor Lee. *Arlington House: Vignettes of a Virginia County*. Arlington: Eleanor Lee Templeman, 1959.

Wilson, Eugene H. Personal Interview. 31 July 1986.

The WPA Guide to Washington, DC. by the Federal Writers' Project. New York: Pantheon Books, 1983.

INDEX

An Act for the Collection of Taxes in Insurrectionary Districts, 27, 136
Alexander, Gerald, 13-14
Algonquin Indians, 11
Ali, Muhammad, 114
American Carriage and Foundry Co., 152
American Expeditionary Forces, 10, 61, 85
American Revolution, 77
Amphitheater, Memorial, 9, 50-54, 65, 73, 81, 86, 111, 112, 114, 137, 138, 150
Andrews Air Force Base, 83
Antietam, Battle of, 37
Apollo I, 10, 139
Aqueduct Bridge, 24, 65
Arc de Triomphe, 61, 62
Argonne Cross, 10, 133
Arlington Heights, 25, 65
Arlington House (Custis-Lee Mansion), 7, 9, 17, 23-24, 27-30, 31, 36, 93, 94, 98, 136, 137, 149
Arlington National Cemetery Map, 134-135
Arlington, sheep shearing, 17
Arlington Village (see Freedman's Village),
Army and Navy Nurses Monument, 133
Arnold, Henry , 131, 149
Armstrong, Philip, 109
Armistice Day, 90
Army of the Republic of Vietnam (ARVN), 72
Arteaga, Jorge, 126
Bakke, Richard, 114
Barrow, Joe Louis Jr., 115
(Barrow), Joe Louis Sr. see Louis, Joe,
Bartlett, Charlie, 94
Batista, Marlo, 80, 131
Beckwith, Robert Todd Lincoln, 56-57
Berkeley, Gov. William, 13
Beruit terrorist bombing, 118-119
Bethesda Naval Hospital, 92
Bicentennial, 111-112, 137
Bigler, Philip, 81
Bird, Samuel, 92-96
Black Jack, 94, 154
Blandy, U.S.S., 69
Block, Harlon, 84
Booth, John Wilkes, 39
Boyington, Pappy, 131
Bradley, John, 84

Bradley, Omar, 131, 139, 149
Bryan, William Jennings, 54, 131
Bull Run, Battle of, 30, 39
Bush, George, 83, 110, 125-126,
burial requirements, 80, 105
Burrows, William, 43
Butler, Benjamin Franklin, 35
caisson platoon, 151-154
Camp Leslie, 25
Canadian Cross, 133
Canberra, U.S.S., 69
caparison (riderless) horse, 153
Capitol rotunda, 70
Carlos, Juan, 111
Carter, Jimmy, 113-114
Cedar of Lebanon, 133
cenotaphs, 106
Chaffee, Roger Bruce, 10, 121-122, 131
Challenger, 123, 125, 129
Challenger Memorial, 125, 133
Chaplin's Memorial, 133
Charette, William, 69
Charlens-sur-Marne, 62
Chennault, Clair, 131
Choiseul Island, 91
Christman, William Henry , 27, 128, 131, 136
Churubusco, Mexico, 37
Civil War, American, 7, 10, 77, 89, 151
Clay, Henry, 19
Cold War, 82
Colon Cemetery, 48
Columbarium, 128, 139
Commerford, John, 41, 131
Confederate Memorial, 10, 44, 133
Cook, Terrence, 103
Costanzo, Raymond, 111, 112, 127, 128, 129
Cote, Peter, 152
Counter, Allen, 118
Cushing, Cardinal Richard, 96, 100
Custis, Daniel, 14
Custis geneology, 13
Custis, George Washington Parke, 7, 15, 18, 32, 136
Custis, John Parke, 14-15, 136
Custis-Lee Mansion (see Arlington House),
Custis, Mary "Molly", 17, 21, 136
Custis, Nelly, 15
Daniels, Josephus, 50
Decoration Day (see Memorial Day),

de Gaulle, Charles, 96
Dewey Circle, 93, 94
Dewey, George, 48, 63
Diggs farm, 44
Dill, Sir John, 80
Doolittle, Jimmy , 131
Doubleday, Abner, 39, 40, 131
Dulles, John Foster, 131
Eagleston, Glenn, 68
Edwards, Johnathan, 126
82nd Airborne, 111
Eisenhower, Dwight D., 69, 72, 154
eligibility requirements, 144-145
Elizabeth II, 111
Ennes, Philip, 109
Epinal American Military Cemetery, 68
Erhard, Ludwig, 96
experimental stone, 133
Ezekiel, Moses, 44
Federalists, 17
Field of the Dead (Section 13), 7, 28, 29
Fish, Hamilton, 62
Fleete, Henry, 12
Forrestal, U.S.S., 106-108
Forrestal, U.S.S. monument, 133
Fort McPherson, Virginia, 24
Fort Monroe, Virginia, 35
Fort Myer, South Post, 105, 138
Fort Myer, Virginia, 75, 82, 152, 154
Fort Sumter, South Carolina, 39
Fort Whipple, Virginia, 24
Frazier, Joe, 114
Fredericksburg, Battle of, 39
Freedman's Bureau, 34
Freedman's Village, Arlington, 34-35, 42,
   150
French and Indian War, 14
full honor funeral, 151
Fuqua, Paul, 94
Gagnon, Rene, 84, 131, 149
Gannon, Matthew, 119
Garfield, James, 55
Gawler's Funeral Home, 92
Gemini program, 121
General Order #11, 35, 136
Genvea Convention, 80, 156
Gettysburg, Battle of, 39
Glenn, John, 103
Grant, Ulysses, 36, 55
Grissom, Virgil "Gus", 10, 121-122, 131
Grosvenor, Melville, 101
Guard change, 77-78
Gulf of Tonkin incident, 70
Guiteau, Charles, 55
Hadfield, George, 16
Hall's knoll, 48
Halsey, William, 131, 149
Hanson, Alexander, 17
Harding, Warren G., 63-66

Harlin, Mary, 55-56
Hayes, Ira, 84, 131, 149
headstone symbols, 146-147
Henson, Matthew, 116-188, 131
Higginbotham, Thurman, 106
"High Flight", 125
Hilberath, Anton, 80, 131
Hill, A.P., 38
Hirohito, Emperor, 111
Holyhood Cemetery, 92
Holmes, Oliver Wendell, 131
Hopper, Grace Murray, 131
Hoover, Herbert, 57
House, James, 43
Howard, O.O., 34
Howsing, Robert, 13, 136
Hume, Paul, 82
Humphrey, Hubert, 102
Hussein, Saddam, 125-126
Iowa, U.S.S., 63
Iran, 10
Iran hostage crisis, 112-114
Iranian Hostage Rescue Mission, 112-114,
   139
Iranian Hostage Rescue Mission
   Monument, 133
Israel, 109
Irwin, James , 131
Iwo Jima, Battle for, 83-84
Jackson Circle, 45
Jackson, Jesse, 114
Jarvis, Gregory, 124
John-Paul II, 82, 139
Johnson, Lyndon B., 70, 95, 100, 101,
   109, 122, 153
Jones, Thomas H., 67
Kearny, Philip, 37-38, 131
Keene, Laura, 55
Kellog, Allan, 73
Kennedy, Edward B. , 100, 102, 103
Kennedy, Jacqueline, 91-98, 101, 148
Kennedy, Joseph, 89, 103
Kennedy, John Jr., 90
Kennedy, John F., 82, 89-94, 96, 101-102,
   106, 121, 129, 130, 138, 148, 149, 154
Kennedy, Patrick, 91, 92, 98
Kennedy, Robert F., 101-104, 129, 139,
   148
Kennedy gravesite(s) inscriptions, 141-
   143
Kennedy, un-named daughter, 98
Keough, Dennis, 119
Khomeini, Ayatullah, 112
Kimball, Ivory, 67
Korean War, 68, 69
Korean War Unknown Soldier, 9, 69, 70,
   138
Kowalchick, Metro, 94, 95
Kuwait, 125

Lafayette, Marquis de, 19, 136
Landsdowne, Zachary, 54, 131
Leahy, William, 131, 149
Lebanon, 10, 118, 119
Lee, George Washington Custis, 32, 41, 137
Lee, "Lighthorse" Harry, 18
Lee, Mary Custis (see Mary Custis),
Lee, Robert E. , 7, 20-21, 23, 29, 30, 31, 38, 94, 114, 136, 138, 149
L'Enfant, Pierre , 44, 131, 137
Le Harve, France, 63
Lexington, Virginia, 136
Liberty Bell 7, 121
Liberty, U.S.S., 108-110
Liberty, U.S.S. monument, 133
Lincoln, Abraham, 23, 25, 27, 38, 54, 93, 148, 154
Lincoln, Abraham "Jack", 55, 56
Lincoln hospital, 27
Lincoln, Mary Todd, 55
Lincoln Memorial, 67
Lincoln, Robert Todd, 54-56, 131, 137
Lincoln, Tad, 55
Lingan, James McCubbin, 18, 131
Logan, John Alexander, 35
Long Bridge, 24, 36
Long Island National Cemetery, 148
Louis, Joe, 114-116, 131
Lyle, Ned, 68
MacArthur, Arthur, 39, 131
MacArthur, Douglas, 39, 154
Madison, James, 17, 18
Magee, John Gillespie, 125
Maine, Mast of the U.S.S. , 10, 49, 52, 81, 82, 93, 133, 138
Maine, U.S.S., 46-48
Manassas, Battle of (see Bull Run),
Mansfield, Mike, 94
Marine Corps Memorial, 83, 84
Marshall, George C., 131, 149
Marshall, Thurgood, 131, 140
Marvin, Lee, 131
McAuliffe, Anthony, 132
McAuliffe, Christa, 123, 124
McClellan, George, 25, 43
McCord, G., 26
McCormack, John, 94
McDowell, Irvin, 24-25
McKinley, William, 46, 48, 136
McNair, Ronald, 124
McNamara, Robert, 93, 94, 103, 109
Mearns, David, 93
Meason, Thomas, 43
Medal of Honor, 39, 66, 83, 112
Meigs, John Rodgers, 33
Meigs, Montgomery, 27, 28, 32, 34, 132
Memorial Amphitheater (see Amphitheater),

Memorial Bridge, 67, 70, 138
Memorial Chapel, 82
Memorial Day, 9, 35, 37, 76, 136-137, 149
Memorial Gateway, 67, 68
Metzler, John C., 129
Metzler, John J. , 86-87, 92, 93, 96, 97, 99, 132
Mexican War, 21
MIA's, 106
Miles' Mausoleum, 149
Military District of Washington, 91
Miller, Glenn, 133
Miller, Paul, 91, 92
Missionary Ridge, Battle of, 39
Mitchell, Billy, 54
Mitchell, John, 132
Monroe, James, 19
Mount Suribaci, 84
Mount Vernon, 14
Mount Washington, 16
Murphy, Audie , 110-111, 112, 132
NASA, 121
National Cathedral, 91
National Geographic Society, 116
National Park Service, 149
National Society of Colonial Dames, 46
Nazis, 81, 83
Necostin Indians, 11-12
Nixon, Richard M., 69, 70, 71, 102, 111
No Greater Love, 119
Oak Ridge Cemetery, 154
Old Amphitheatre, 38
"Old Bob", 154
Olympia, U.S.S., 63, 64
O'Neil, Edward, 68
Onizuka, Ellison, 124
Ord, Edward, 43
"Old Guard," 3d U.S. Infantry, 9, 75, 152
Paderewski, Ignace, 80-83, 138, 139
Paine, Halbert E., 37
Parks, James, 132
Peary gravesite, 117
Peary, Robert, 116, 132
Pei, I.M., 103
Pershing, John J., 10, 63, 64, 85-87, 132, 138
Persian Gulf War, 125, 140
Plenty Coup, Chief, 64, 66
Powers, David, 89, 91, 101
Powers, Francis Gary, 132, 139
Prudenza, Archangelo, 80, 132
PT-59, 91
PT-109, 148
Punchbowl National Cemetery, 68
Quezon, Manuel, 81, 138
Randolph, John , 19
Randolph, Mary Ann, 20
Randolph, Wallace Fitz, 33, 132

Reagan, Ronald, 73, 105, 114-115, 118
Reed, Walter, 132
Reinhardt, Levi, 34
Resnick, Judith, 124
Reynolds, Frank, 132
Rich, Lorimer, 67, 132
Rickover, Hyman, 132
Ridgeway, Matthew , 132
Robertson, James, 93
Robinson, Roscoe, 132
Romagne Cemetery, 63
Roosevelt, Franklin, 81, 148,
Roosevelt Gate, 67
Roosevelt, Theodore, 57, 58, 59
Rosecrans, William Starke , 132
Rosenthal, Joe, 84
Rough Riders Memorial, 133
Ross, Robert, 18
Rossi, Marie Therese, 127, 132
San Joaquin Valley National Cemetery,
    149
Schley Gate, 67
Schley, Winfield Scott, 67
Scobee, Francis Dick, 10, 124, 132, 139
Scobee, June, 124
Scott, Winfield, 23, 38
Secret Service, 92
Section 1, 33, 39
Section 7A, 124
Section 13, 32
Section 15, 80
Section 27, 35
Section 46, 108, 114, 124, 139
Section 59, 119
Selfridge, Thomas, 49, 50, 123, 132, 137
Selassie, Haile, 96
Sentinel's Creed, 78
Serpens Memorial, 133
Shaw, Timothy, 126, 127
Shenandoah, 53, 54
Shepard, Alan, 121
Sheridan, Philip, 10, 34, 43, 132
Shriver, Sargent, 91, 92
Sickles, Daniel , 132
Sirhan, Sirhan, 102
Smith, John, 11-12, 136
Smith, Michael , 10, 124, 132, 139
Solomon Islands, 91
Sousley, Franklin, 84
Spanish-American War, 10, 46, 49, 137
Spanish-American War Memorial, 133
Stanton, Edwin, 27, 39
Stethem, Robert, 119, 132
Strank, Michael, 84, 132, 149
Stewart, Potter, 132
Sullivan Mausoleum, 149
Swan, Caleb, 43
Taft, William Howard, 10, 49, 57, 64, 91,
    132, 137, 149

Tanner, James, 38, 132
Tansill, X. Bender, 109
"Taps", 7
Taylor, Maxwell , 103, 132
Texas, U.S.S., 48
tier burial, 105
Tomb Guard, 75-76
Tomb Guard Badge, 76
Tomb of the Unknown Soldier, 9, 76, 86,
    111, 116, 124, 138, 139, 149
traffic, 106
Triband, P. Regis, 24
Truman, Harry S, 86
Tsantes, George, 119
2,111 Unknowns Memorial, 7, 31, 133,
    136
Unknown Soldier, Korea, 68-72, 138
Unknown Soldier, World War I, 9, 61-67,
    137
Unknown Soldier, World War II, 9, 67-72,
    73, 138
Unknown Soldier, Vietnam, 70-75, 139
United States Colored Troops, 35
Van Fleet, James A., 132
Veterans' Administration, 111, 149
Veterans' Day, 148
Vietnam War, 9, 10, 72, 106-108 115
Villa, Franciso "Pancho", 85
Wainwright, Jonathan, 114
Walter Reed Army Hospital, 85
War of 1812, 17, 18, 137
War of 1812 Unknowns, 133
Warren, Earl, 10, 94, 132
Warnecke, John, 100
Washington College, 29, 31
Washington Navy Yard, 64
Washington, George, 14-15, 54
Washington, Martha, 15
Washington Monument, 21
Wehle, Philip, 90
Weinberger, Caspar, 73, 114
Weitzel, Godfrey, 43
Welesa, Lech, 82
Westminster Abbey, 61, 62
West Point, 123
White, Edward, 121, 122
Wilson, Eugene, 94
Wilson, Michael, 152
Wilson, Woodrow, 44, 45, 50, 51, 53, 57,
    64, 65, 91, 148
Wojtyla, Karol (see John-Paul II),
Women in Military Service Memorial, 128
Woodlawn Cemetery, 118
World War I, 61-64, 85
World War II, 67, 79, 114
Wright, Orville, 49, 137
Yalta Conference, 81
Younger, Edward F., 62, 63, 133